"Think re-materialization, not
  de-materialization.

Life is based on materials — literally.
Let's celebrate that fact."[2]

# The Materials Book

### Edited by
### Ilka Ruby & Andreas Ruby

# The Matter of Construction: Systemic Overhaul or Tweaking the Status Quo?

## Introduction by
## Marc Angélil and Cary Siress

We know the images. Whether under construction or plotted well into the future, one grandiose real estate project after another is endorsed as a vision of prosperity beyond dispute, each following the unspoken truism: "Everything that appears is good; whatever is good will appear."[1] Never mind that the bulk of such projects, though marketed as unique, usually look the same regardless of where they land. Also, pay no heed to the lack of rationale for ever more lavish properties, since supply always manages to trump need. In this ongoing wager, ends are nothing; capital accumulation and circulation are all, and the only thing these visions plan to develop is themselves. The hypnotic call for growth would seem to convey little or no concern for material constraints, considering that excessive volume and speed persevere in the hurried pursuit of more and more profitable construction venues. And so, those increasingly fraught debates rage on about how best to meet market demands for the ever further expansion of the built environment while also devising more sustainable ways of building. The necessity for change appears obvious, but how to implement it remains, for the most part, obscure. It is thus no wonder that the ruse of development for development's sake still holds sway, at times addressed head-on and thus brought out of hiding, only to be relegated to the margins once again as other more pressing matters fill the room.[2]

While executives in the building industry may differ in their approach to monitoring the impact of the latest business venture, most everyone concerned about the matter of construction agrees that the material intensity of mainstream building practices is unsustainable. The construction sector not only uses an exorbitant amount of resources, it is also responsible for the use of material compounds that are harmful to humans and the environment. Considering material quantity and quality as well as the amount of energy consumed by buildings over their entire use cycle, it is apparent that more environmentally mindful and socially responsible protocols could lower emissions and reduce dependence on resource extraction from the natural environment and at the same time minimize widespread health risks.

Need it be said that the ecological footprint of the construction industry must be urgently addressed? Although increasing energy efficiency and the use of renewable energy sources has made headway as an obvious first step, and even though green, smart, and eco-friendly rhetoric is as routine as it is abundant, it is now high time to foreground material stocks and flows in order to further the objectives, long overdue, of truly sustainable construction. In the face of looming climate-borne catastrophes, the building industry's cumulative effects on the environment are too significant to be conveniently ignored any longer, and the construction sector figures as a key site to leverage transformation in how we build and what gets built. Construction, in so many words, is viewed as both the *problem* and the *solution*.

An intense debate arises when it comes to reducing the use of building materials or devising alternative approaches. Some argue for the outright "dematerialization" of construction, a drastic reduction in the amount of physical substance that goes into the built environment — in essence, "doing more and more with less and less until eventually you can do everything with nothing," as provocatively put forth by R. Buckminster Fuller some time ago.[3] Others push back by proposing a discourse on "re-materializing" construction, a twofold pathway toward reframing the entire sector by promoting both building materials that have little impact on the environment and the repeated reuse of materials after their conventional use cycle.[4] If nothing else, this debate highlights the wicked problem of gains in resource leanness and ecological soundness being nullified by ever-increasing material volumes required to fulfill ever-increasing demands—a catch-22 of global proportions that sees improvements in sustainable practices being offset by demographic growth and the mounting desire for higher living standards that comes with the urbanization of society.

Although there is little disagreement about the need for action, there is a correlated debate about whether it should be made in small or big steps — as radical or incremental change. Those promoting a broad paradigm shift in the use of materials back the stance of William McDonough and Michael Braungart, who proclaim that "being less bad is simply not good enough," as if to assert that little changes here and there simply will not meet the challenges at hand.[5] Taking this cue, proponents for big change insist on fundamentally rethinking and "remaking the way we make things," as stated by the subtitle of their seminal 2002 book, *Cradle to Cradle*. On the other hand, advocates for step-by-step adjustments claim that such sweeping measures will require overbearing, top-down mandates that in the end might override local concerns altogether. What's more, radical change, they maintain, will most likely necessitate extensive research and trials before being implemented. They further argue that the advantage of incremental transformations is that they can be pursued immediately with less risk by incorporating all known gains, however marginal.[6] Thus, though both sides acknowledge that change is of paramount importance, differences linger regarding its scope and pace. Whatever the answer, be it systemic overhaul or tweaking the status quo, it remains clear to all that we do not have the luxury of time in deciding how to act.

Another clash concerns whether the call for durability of materials is compatible with sustaining the economy. If materials were designed to endure far beyond a standard use cycle, then the resulting reduction of material flows could trigger economic stagnation, in turn negatively affecting the industry, as well as society at large. Although it might seem the most obvious option for bringing about effective change in how we make things, material permanence nevertheless has a downside.[7] Making the physical stuff of the built environment do more for longer not only disregards the current market logic's continuous demand for new products, it also seems to overlook the evolution of needs and uses over time. The issue of bringing durability in line with the constant of change has given rise to discussions on mining the city for reusable stocks, on market platforms for buying and selling used building components, and on design for the disassembly and reuse of parts, in effect calling attention to the undervalued notion of the built environment as a stockpile of valuable resources. Whereas some claim that built structures must be considered in terms of the different rates of decay of their constituent elements and systems, others defend the maxim "never demolish, always transform," and contend that getting the most from the turnover of the built fabric far outweighs the commonplace practice of forever constructing anew.[8] That said, the push for circular construction ultimately requires a thorough retooling of the market itself in view of the long-term returns of circular economies.

Disagreements do have their benefits. Acknowledging that construction is both the problem, with regard to unsustainable modes of development, and the solution, with regard to devising ways to sustain human-made and natural environments, propositions have been drafted that provide much-needed guidance for industry leaders and policymakers alike.[9] Hardly uncontroversial or contradiction-free, these propositions pertain to innovations in the material sector and range from the promotion of circular metabolisms to the elimination of the concept of waste; from detoxification to the binding reduction of greenhouse-gas emissions; from minimizing the use of materials to maximizing their functionalities; from prohibiting precarious building techniques to expanding the development and deployment of clean technologies; from reducing the construction sector's footprint to increasing the local social benefits of building practices worldwide. If all such propositions were implemented, the ways and means of construction could be reoriented along regenerative pathways that are crucial to maintaining sustainability as the modus operandi of the industry. And who knows, perhaps these propositions might also inform those spokespeople for the "good life" whose spectacularly generic development projects are meant to invoke the spell of development for development's sake again and again whenever the matter of construction is debated. Let's hope so. If not, countless other rank-and-file administrators—along with private-sector investors and developers from near and far—will no doubt feel duty-bound to proceed with business as usual. Should that be the agenda, we may very well be in store for many more failed spectacles scattered across the globe—overly expensive, without use, and unsustainable. But with the clock ticking for us all, they too will have to finally cede to reality—for in our current predicament, "no one, after all, can be in favor of 'unsustainability.'"[10]

Admittedly, such shifts in mindsets and practices are a tall order. Nevertheless it is to these urgent ends that this publication is committed. The varied subject matter that follows was debated at the 6th International LafargeHolcim Forum, "Re-materializing Construction," held at the American University in Cairo in April 2019 and organized by the LafargeHolcim Foundation for Sustainable Construction. The objective of the conference was to provide a platform for exchange among researchers and practitioners in the construction sector, with the aim of fostering whole-system thinking and proposing solutions to reposition construction as a crucial driver of change. The keynote addresses were delivered by Lord Norman Foster, Christine Binswanger, Anne Lacaton, Francis Kéré, Laila Iskandar, Simon Upton, Michael Braungart, and Mitchell Joachim. The conference was structured according to interrelated topics of material deployment in construction, the ambition being to make all associated practices within the industry sustainable. Workshops were moderated by Marilyne Andersen, Philippe Block, Harry Gugger, Guillaume Habert, Dirk Hebel, Anna Heringer, Karen Scrivener, and Werner Sobek. The "22 Propositions" were compiled and edited by Sarah Nichols.

We are thankful to all of them for their valuable contributions. In addition, deep appreciation goes to Edi Schwarz from the LafargeHolcim Foundation in Zurich, as well as to Ilka Ruby, Andreas Ruby, Max Bach, and Something Fantastic in Berlin, who edited, designed, and produced the book. Sincere gratitude is also extended to all participants, whose work has contributed to bringing the sustainable materialization of the built environment to the forefront of academic and professional debates on best practices in the industry and beyond.

1   Guy Debord, *The Society of the Spectacle*, trans. Donald Nicholson-Smith (New York: Zone Books, 1994), xx; originally published as *La société du spectacle* (Paris: Buchet-Chastel, 1967).

2   Comment by Alejandro Aravena in a panel discussion with Christine Binswanger, Lord Norman Foster, and Maria Atkinson, 6th International LafargeHolcim Forum for Sustainable Construction, American University in Cairo, April 4, 2019.

3   R. Buckminster Fuller, *Nine Chains to the Moon* (New York: Anchor Books, 1938), 252. For the notion of dematerialization, see Vaclav Smil, *Making the Modern World: Materials and Dematerialization* (West Sussex: John Wiley & Sons, 2014).

4   For the use of the term re-materialization, see William McDonough and Michael Braungart, "Reinventing the World: Step Four," *Green@Work*, September–October 2001, 31.

5   William McDonough and Michael Braungart, *Cradle to Cradle: Remaking the Way We Make Things* (New York: North Point Press, 2002), 45.

6   These points were made by Simon Upton regarding the debates between what he called "incrementalists" and "radical change exponents," email to the authors, April 11, 2019.

7   Smil, *Making the Modern World*, 177.

8   Frédéric Druot, Anne Lacaton, and Jean-Philippe Vassal, *Plus: Large Scale Housing Developments — An Exceptional Case* (Barcelona: Editorial Gustavo Gili, 2007), 29.

9   See Sarah Nichols, ed., *Re-materializing Construction: 22 Propositions* (Zurich: LafargeHolcim Foundation for Sustainable Construction, 2019).

10  David Harvey, "What's Green and Makes the Environment Go Round?," in *The Cultures of Globalization*, ed. Fredric Jameson and Masao Miyoshi (Durham, NC: Duke University Press, 1998), 337.

# 22 Propositions for Re-materializing Construction

## Edited by
## Sarah Nichols

Propositions 1–22

The propositions were debated
in a series of roundtable
discussions organized by
the LafargeHolcim Foundation
for Sustainable Construction
from 2014 to 2018 and were
edited by Sarah Nichols.

Participants

Marilyne Andersen
Marc Angélil
Alejandro Aravena
Annette Aumann
Xuemei Bai
Philippe Block
Michael Braungart
Dominique Corvez
Jens Diebold
Heike Faulhammer
John Fernández
Maarten Gielen
Harry Gugger
Guillaume Habert
Dirk Hebel
Anna Heringer
Mark Jarzombek
Reed Kroloff
Vivian Loftness
Sarah Nichols
John Ochsendorf
Werner Oechslin
Susan Parnell
Shrashtant Patara
Karen Scrivener
Laila Seewang
Werner Sobek
Mark Swilling

"Being less bad
is simply not good enough." [1]

Building depends on materials—a
lot of them. The construction sector
uses two-fifths of all gravel and sand
as well as a quarter of the virgin
wood consumed in the world. It is
also responsible for 40 percent of
energy and 20 percent of water used
globally. If tomorrow's cities are built
like today's cities, business-as-usual
material protocols will have serious
and possibly irreparable costs for
the environment. Using less a little
bit better cannot offset the increases
projected for expanding cities.

Yet within this potentially troubling
scenario there is also possibility: since
construction uses significant amounts
of material—and will likely soon use
even more—rethinking materials and

material use also has tremendous potential to lower greenhouse gas emissions and reduce dependence on resource extraction.

The following propositions aim to "re-materialize" construction by rethinking the building-material cycle from extraction to processing, design, transport, installation, maintenance, and removal. It is hoped that changes such as those proposed here would lead to a construction industry with a smaller ecological footprint and a shift away from the unsustainable assumption that raw materials are infinitely available. Thinking further, what if there were no trade-offs between costs and benefits—could we make materials that are only beneficial? While alternate futures can and should be imagined, from the perspective of the world we inhabit today, providing good materials in sufficient quantities is a major challenge. Supplying the comforts that materials can provide—shelter from the elements, privacy, a place in the world—while at the same time reducing harm requires careful consideration of the political, economic, social, and energy frameworks in which the building trade is situated. As such, many of the material shifts proposed here also presuppose immaterial changes to the business of material supply, construction, and real estate. Put simply, though the focus here is on materials, the material and immaterial are inseparable.

The fact is that a diverse planet will require diverse solutions—that the right solution in one situation may be harmful in another. The first proposition, for example, was hotly debated but is ultimately included as a familiar starting point for thinking about materials. The propositions range from pragmatic to utopian, in acknowledgment of the fact that perhaps tactics that can be applied today and long-term strategies for systemic change are both needed.

1 Michael Braungart and William McDonough, *Cradle to Cradle: Remaking the Way We Make Things* (New York: North Point Press, 2002), 45.

# 1
# "How Much Does Your Building Weigh, Mr. Foster?"[1]

R. Buckminster Fuller posed this question, used as the title of a recent documentary, as Norman Foster showed him designs for the ultra-lightweight Sainsbury Gallery at the University of East Anglia. The question implies that lighter is better—and that reducing the amount of material in a project also reduces the embodied energy of a given structure. This principle is useful to apply in an apples-to-apples scenario: a building with less steel will probably have less embodied energy than a building with more steel.

However, in an apples-to-oranges scenario, this principle can be misleading. A lightweight steel-and-glass structure does not necessarily have less embodied energy than heavy masonry. Some lightweight materials require high energy expenditure for their production, others do not. Timber may be both lightweight and low energy, while aluminum is lightweight and recyclable but energy-intensive. It may be useful to think of material use in terms of performance: What is the minimum of any given material needed to perform a certain function, and how would another material's performance compare?

1 *How Much Does Your Building Weigh, Mr. Foster?*, Norberto Lopez Amado and Carlos Carcas, Art Commissioners, documentary, 2010.

# 2
# Know Your Materials

What materials are in this building? Where did they come from?

These simple questions are not always easy for designers, clients, consultants, and contractors to answer. Yet, rethinking material use in buildings is predicated on being able to answer such questions. To re-materialize construction we have to know our materials. And knowing our materials isn't a simple matter at all.

How was the material produced?

Who made it, and under what conditions?

What by-products were incidentally made along with it?

What happened to those by-products?

How did the material arrive to the site?

How long will it last?

Will it behave as predicted or as promised?

What can be done with it afterward?

Could I eat it?

Knowing materials means asking more questions. This is the first step to understanding business as usual, finding alternatives within the present system, and inventing future alternatives.

# 3
# Do Not Forget CO$_2$

The construction sector is directly or indirectly responsible for approximately half of all global CO$_2$ emissions. Carbon dioxide is produced at every stage of a structure's use cycle.

Building material production is a significant source of CO$_2$ emissions. Cement production releases 5 to 7 percent of all anthropogenic CO$_2$ emissions. Steel for construction may represent another 5 percent of CO$_2$ emissions. These represent significant areas for improvement, though reducing CO$_2$ output needs to be balanced with improving resource efficiency—two aims that are sometimes in conflict with one another.

Building operations are also a significant source of carbon dioxide. Heating buildings emits about 20 percent of all anthropogenic carbon dioxide, and most of these emissions are produced in the northern hemisphere. Though this is in large part a question of which sources are used to supply energy, it is also a material question (at least until a total shift is made to renewable, non-harmful energy sources!).

Putting thermal mass to use, insulating, or even reflecting upon thermal-comforts standards (wearing a sweater is easier than renovating a facade) may all be pathways to reducing the CO$_2$ output from heating through buildings. Cooling buildings currently produces comparatively less carbon dioxide than heating but is expected to increase. In general, low-income regions use less energy because of the prohibitive cost of energy. In Brazil, for example, only 2 percent of CO$_2$ emissions are associated with building use—and this is mostly for cooking.

# 4
# Produce
# Leaner

What if all the matter extracted for building materials was used somewhere in the supply chain? To mine resources much more mass is extracted from the earth—typically two to three times more—than the amount used. For some resources, as a deposit is quarried, this ratio continues to increase, requiring more and more extraction for the same output.

Reuse of by-products is already part of the material supply chain. Timber production, for example, incorporates several forms of reuse. Shavings are used to produce particleboard, and sawdust can be used to fire kilns used in the lumber-drying process.

Improving the production chain of building materials could greatly reduce the amount of raw materials consumed by urbanization, increasing material efficiency. Or, perhaps the question should be stated more radically: Could materials be produced without any raw-material extraction at all? Higher material efficiency could have advantages for all actors. Reduced material costs could be an incentive for manufacturers to improve product supply chains—savings that should be passed on to users.

# 5
# Supply Better

What if all the materials on a construction site were used? The last step, from manufacturer to building, offers significant possibilities for reducing material use. How materials are handled on-site and how they reach the site could both be improved.

Most construction materials are relatively inexpensive compared to the cost of transportation. Contractors in many different places use large overage estimates to ensure that the basic materials needed are readily available on-site. When extra material is not used, it often becomes waste. Improper storage, damage during transportation, cutting to size, and mixing materials like plaster on-site all contribute to construction-site waste, which is often estimated to be around 10 percent. For some projects, this figure is perhaps far higher: recent studies of Brazilian construction sites show that median wastage rates for cement and aggregates can be as high as 45 percent.[1] More accurate estimating practices and training to improve on-site handling of materials could significantly reduce the amount of waste created by delivery and construction. Reclaiming and reusing offcuts and excess would further improve material use on-site.

1 United Nations Environment Programme, *Eco-efficient Cements: Potential Economically Viable Solutions for a Low-CO2 Cement-Based Materials Industry* (Paris: UNEP, 2016), 24.

# 6
# What Is
# the Labor Cost?

Making materials and assembling them requires labor. In evaluating material choice, the working conditions for producing a material should be part of the equation, from raw-material extraction to the factory and construction site.

Even materials that look and perform identically may have been produced under wildly different conditions. Workers have the right to a safe, equitable, and healthy work environment, and workers should be employed with a living wage, health care, and fair contracts; materials produced without these conditions are not sustainable. In the construction industry, however, these conditions are often not met—most construction work worldwide is carried out as day labor or under temporary or informal contracts.[1]

The place where work for a construction site comes from should also be considered. If construction creates employment within the community, projects have an immediate local benefit through the influx of wages and the potential introduction of new skills. If work is done remotely or workers have been transported to the site, under what conditions has it been conducted, and on what grounds?

1 Jill Wells, "Informality in the Construction Sector in Developing Countries," *Construction Management* 25, no.1 (2007): 87–93.

# 7
# Is the Price Right?

What if producers and consumers were responsible for the full impact of materials? Currently, material prices don't take costs to the environment, labor, and finite resource stocks into full account. In the book *A History of the World in Seven Cheap Things*, Raj Patel and Jason W. Moore argue that many undervalued elements—from lives to nature—lead to commodities being priced below their full impact.[1]

Human and environmental costs are generated by a material during extraction, production, and installation, but also during de-montage, removal, and recycling. If life-cycle accounting were reflected in material pricing, the actual impact of material use would be more evident to consumers. Prices that reflect the full environmental cost of production, use, and disposal could help make material use more sustainable.[2]

A recycling tax modeled on electronic-waste recycling fees could provide one possibility. In places like Switzerland, the European Union, and California, consumers pay a nominal surcharge for future electronics recycling at the moment of purchase, and California also uses a similar model for mattresses, for instance. Could something similar work for building components? What price should we set for the value of coming generations to have access to the same environmental quality and resources?

1 Raj Patel and Jason W. Moore, *A History of the World in Seven Cheap Things* (Berkeley: University of California Press, 2018).

2 Friedrich Schmidt-Bleek, *Future: Beyond Climatic Change* (Carnoules, France: Factor Ten Institute, 2008), 9.

# 8
# Build Local
# Material Industries

Using locally sourced materials—whether high- or low-tech—holds a number of social and economic benefits, and may also reduce the energy costs of transportation. In places where not all materials are available, this may mean prioritizing materials according to local availability and encouraging the development of local material industries. Developing countries still rely heavily on building-material imports. In Ethiopia, for example, more than 80 percent of construction material is imported.[1]

While local material use reduces emissions and the expenditure of fossil fuels for transportation, this may be offset by less clean manufacturing—the embodied energy of concrete produced in Switzerland is lower than that of concrete produced in Brazil, for example. Thus, local material use will not always immediately result in a savings of embodied energy. Investing in local industry can, though, eventually give material supply chains the economic basis to become cleaner, making a long-term positive change to a community's material flow.

1 Dirk Hebel, "The Vernacular Rediscovered: Applying Local Construction Technologies and Materials in Ethiopia," in *Reinventing Construction*, ed. Ilka & Andreas Ruby (Berlin: Ruby Press, 2010), 311.

# 9
# Mine
# the City

The city is a rich material resource; for example, there is more copper in buildings than is left in the earth's crust. In Switzerland, the total copper stock in buildings is 65 kg per capita.[1] By reusing the materials already deposited in our settlements rather than extracting new raw materials, the rate of material accumulation would slow down and the amount of building materials removed and redeposited as waste would be reduced.

Formally or informally, we already mine the city. In parts of the United States, copper extraction from abandoned and inhabited buildings is so lucrative that police task forces have been formed to combat metal theft. But the institutions needed to effectively mine the city are presently missing. The labor needed to sort and select materials for reuse needs an economic apparatus.

Presently, although the labor of erecting new buildings is a crucial part of the economy, demolishing them is often done haphazardly and with a minimum of time and labor.

1 Peter Baccini and Alejandra Pedraza, "Die Bestimmung von Materialgehalten in Gebäuden," in *Bauwerke als Ressourcennutzer und Ressourcenspender in der langfristigen Entwicklung urbaner Systeme: Ein Beitrag zur Exploration urbaner Lagerstätten* (Zurich: vdf, 2006), 103–32.

# 10
# Maintain or Renew, Reuse or Recycle?

When does it make sense to stick with an existing building, and when to renew it? When does it make sense to use a new material versus reusing or recycling an existing one? For buildings, the energy costs of existing construction can be weighed against potential savings with renovations or new construction.

Similarly, the benefits of reusing and recycling materials can be weighed against other factors like potential reductions in material performance. Recycled aggregates in concrete, for example, have lower performance than natural ones, which can lead to additional cement in the concrete mix, thereby increasing the resource efficiency of the aggregate but also increasing the $CO_2$ output of the concrete as a whole. Jonathan Cullen frames it as follows: "Two guiding questions to ask when assessing end-of-life options for waste materials or products are: how much energy is required to restore the recovered material back to the desired material or product? And, how does this quantity compare with obtaining the desired material or product from virgin or primary sources?"[1]

1 Jonathan M. Cullen, "Circular Economy: Theoretical Benchmark or Perpetual Motion Machine?," *Journal of Industrial Ecology* 21, no. 3 (2017): 483–86.

# 11
# Designing for Nontoxicity: "Could I Eat Your Furniture, IKEA?"[1]

What if materials were not just nontoxic but also regenerative—could a building clean the air? Titanium-dioxide facade coatings are being studied for pollution capture and a range of studies are underway on carbon sequestration in common materials.

Designing for nontoxicity is a first step toward regeneration that can be taken today. Materials that contain chemicals hazardous to human or environmental health are not recyclable, create enduring waste, may harm the workers producing them, and may emit hazardous chemicals—especially if they catch fire.

Some of the most common building materials are made from hazardous materials. PVC (used for pipes), polyurethane (insulation), resin (flooring), formaldehyde (plywood), flame retardants, petrochemical-based products, heavy-metal additives (used in many products like sealants), and persistent bio-accumulative toxics (PBTs), like chlorine, are all harmful. Chemicals in hazardous materials travel down and upstream, and some, like PBTs, only break down after long periods of time.

1 Vivian Loftness, 2nd LafargeHolcim Roundtable, 2015.

# 12
# Simplify
# Material Labels

Revealing the impacts that our material needs have is an important first step toward allowing design professionals, companies, and global citizens to make informed choices. What if the life-cycle costs and embodied energy of materials were clearly communicated to make the impact of different options comparable?

Currently there are many competing material labels that offer complex metrics unintelligible to many consumers. The standard nutrition labels on food packaging may provide an alternative model to consider; something similar has been proposed with the "Declare" material label. Certainly, material performance under different site and programmatic conditions is more difficult to calculate and convey than caloric values. Still, labels may provide a rough but useful measuring stick.

The aim of unified labeling should be simplicity, transparency, and legibility for all consumers. What if labels were so clear that the informal sector could also be well informed about their material choices?

# 13
# Cross
# Loops

What if building materials became nutrients for biological or technical cycles? Cradle-to-cradle thinking proposes redesigning building materials so they can be reused or repurposed after they are reclaimed from buildings, creating value and products out of used material. Materials could be biodegradable or endlessly recyclable—resources that are used and reused rather than discarded and then extracted or produced anew.[1]

In addition to the cyclical logic of recycling, materials could also loop back into other cycles of production. Building materials that break down into agricultural and industrial nutrients would help eliminate waste. Textiles or fiber panels can be designed to biodegrade so that they can be reused as nutrients. Other materials like glass and aluminum can be designed to be recycled multiple times, though the energy intensity of the recycling process needs to be taken into account. Cycling can work in both directions: just as construction components could be transformed into agricultural nutrients, packaging, industrial, or agricultural by-products could become building materials.

1 Michael Braungart, "Upcycle to Eliminate Waste," *Nature* 494 (February 14, 2013): 174.

# 14
# Create Building-Component Exchanges

What if building components were sold and resold and resold again? To reuse building materials, they need to be recovered, inspected, stored, and resold. Institutions that make this exchange, verification, and revaluing possible could be exciting new actors in the material supply chain.

Building-component exchange companies survey buildings that are to be demolished or renovated and assess the feasibility of reclaiming components; act as experts in carefully extracting and transporting the materials; sort, clean, and store the components; and build a client pool of contractors and designers to whom they can resell. Their role as guarantors for the resold components is equally important. Without a legal entity that can be held liable in the event of failure, building components—especially structural assemblies that need to be retested—often cannot be reused.

Specifications also play an important role in facilitating or hindering reuse. They could be assessed and potentially rewritten to enable the use of reclaimed materials wherever possible by, for example, allowing for irregular lengths.[1]

1 Maarten Gielen, lecture at ETH Zurich, April 1, 2015.

# 15
# Imagine a World without Waste

What if waste did not exist? This sounds like a utopian idea in today's economy, but waste as we know it is a relatively new concept. Waste is tied to the idea of consumption: commodities are purchased, used, and then discarded. A world of consumers has exploded the amount of waste and produced types of waste that would be unfamiliar to previous generations. Understanding that business as usual is not the natural order of things helps generate alternatives. Perhaps even just redefining the words we use to talk about material flows can also help redefine the infrastructures that produce and move materials.

Eliminating the idea of waste suggests producing leaner, supplying better, mining the city, crossing loops, and exchanging building components. In short, it summarizes the idea of employing all strategies at once — nose-to-tail production (no waste in the production stream), reuse (circular within one sector), and cradle-to-cradle (looping between sectors, upcycling and downcycling) — while also providing a larger vision for all of them.

# 16
# Match
# Use Span

What if we made materials do more by using them longer? In *Making the Modern World*, Vaclav Smil proposed that "design for durability is perhaps the most obvious option."[1] Durability, however, would require a reformulation of the building economy, which currently makes buildings obsolescent far before buildings and infrastructures reach the end of their use cycles.

It may be useful to think about matching the durability of materials to the projected use span of a building. Will a building be in use for 200 years, forty years, twenty years, or two months?

Do the amount of materials used and their expected service life make sense? A building's projected use span should affect the materials it uses and how they are assembled. In some cases, projects can and should be designed for longevity and use durable materials that also ensure the maintenance needed to keep them operational can be carried out.

It is also important to understand how user needs will change over time and whether these needs will generate new or different demands. For some functions, adaptability can be built-in, allowing a structure to perform beyond the lifespan of its given use. For others, a project can be built with the intention of growth so that additional space and material is only used if and when it is called for and when the inhabitants are able to pay for the expansion.

1 Vaclav Smil, *Making the Modern World: Materials and Dematerialization* (Chichester, UK: John Wiley, 2014).

# 17
# Design for Disassembly

What if we eliminated the idea of demolition? Until the beginning of the twentieth century, it was commonplace for buildings to be unbuilt and their parts sorted, reclaimed, and reused. This provides a powerful example of how to think of buildings as a stockpile of materials instead of as future waste.

Composite materials are particularly difficult to reuse because their individual components cannot be recovered. Similarly, using insoluble adhesives make building products difficult to reuse.

If materials can be easily recovered, they are more likely to be reused. Whenever possible, materials should be combined in ways where they can be re-separated or reused as an assembly, using screws or nails or even magnets and hooks. Temporary structures could be built entirely as components. Like a circus tent, Olympic venues or exhibition halls could be moveable pop-ups instead of fixed buildings, appearing when and where they are needed.

# 18
# Never Demolish, Always Transform

"It's a matter of never demolishing, subtracting or replacing things, but always adding, transforming and utilizing them."[1]

How much of a building needs to change along with uses and desires? Most modern buildings last between twelve and fifty years.[2] During that time, renovations often also lead to additional material turnover. What if buildings took adaptation into account from the beginning?

Simple architectural strategies could extend the usable lifespan of buildings. Buildings can be designed to be as neutral as possible, with dimensions, partitions, and circulation that can host different activities without much change. Buildings can also be designed as frames that facilitate changes to the interior or the facade. Any change removes and adds some material, but changing a part is less effort than unbuilding a whole building and rebuilding anew.

1 Frédéric Druot, Anne Lacaton, and Jean-Philippe Vassal, *Plus: Large Scale Housing Developments—An Exceptional Case* (Barcelona: Editorial Gustavo Gili, 2007), 29.

2 Vaclav Smil, *Making the Modern World: Materials and Dematerialization* (Chichester, UK: John Wiley, 2014), 110.

# 19
# Rightsize

Much of the world still needs better housing. As their needs are met, it may be useful to reflect on the standards of the developed world. Is bigger always better? As living standards increase, the average area per inhabitant for living space, working space, and infrastructure also grows.[1] The most notable changes have been in housing, as area has grown while household size has shrunk. The average area of a new American home increased from 154 square meters in 1973 to 234 square meters in 2007.[2]

An increase in building volume typically requires more structural materials, creates larger surfaces for finishes, and needs more energy for heating, cooling, lighting, and appliances. These increases may be mitigated through efficient structural design, sustainable materials, and renewable energy sources. Larger living spaces can also create a barrier to using higher performance or more sustainable materials because the cost of upgrading gets multiplied by the additional area. Smaller spaces can thus be a direct way to reduce material intensity and lower the barrier for using quality materials.

1 Alex Wilson and Jessica Boehland, "Small Is Beautiful: US House Size, Resource Use and the Environment," *Journal of Industrial Ecology* 9 (January 2005): 277–87.

2 Jonathan Massey, "Risk and Regulation in the Financial Architecture of American Houses," in *Governing by Design: Architecture, Economy, and Politics*, ed. Aggregate (Pittsburgh: University of Pittsburgh Press, 2012), 40.

# 20
# Embed Know-How

Construction can create social and microeconomic value. Using local building techniques or teaching new ones to a community can introduce or help maintain craftsmanship within a community—and maintain the notion of community itself. When know-how remains local and the necessary tools are available, communities can maintain, rebuild, adjust, or expand according to their needs. If local or vernacular construction also addresses climate regulation passively, long-term savings on energy expenditure may also be a benefit.

Techniques that require periodic maintenance, like rammed earth, stone masonry, or thatched roof construction, keep know-how alive through regular cycles of repair. Each maintenance cycle can be used to train new laborers and is income for local workers. As long as know-how remains, what is treasured can be maintained for generations and new projects can also employ the same techniques.

By using local techniques, there is less dependence on external materials and expertise, promoting self-sufficiency. If a project uses unfamiliar techniques, strategies for passing on and maintaining knowledge and standards will also be important parts of the design. Transmitting new techniques may also require unconventional, nontechnical forms of representation or communication.

# 21
# Make It
# Desirable

Desire is a powerful mobilizer —sometimes stronger than duty or responsibility. If products and buildings that reduce the material cost of building are desirable, they are more likely to catch on with a wider public. Adding beauty, convenience, or novelty to a project can help transform sustainability from something that subtracts to something that adds.

The food industry provides a reference for how to tap into the force of desire. People are willing to pay a higher price for a sustainable, organic, pesticide-free tomato not only because it is more sustainable but because it tastes better. Science and technology may develop new, very efficient, low-carbon-footprint materials, but unless they are cheaper, faster, or easier to use than conventional ones, they are not going to be preferred. In order to promote sustainable materials with the strong force of immediate gratification, we should find a way to make the joy of them more tangible.

Proposition 23-37

# 22

# "If Less Is More, Maybe Nothing Is Everything"[1]

Construction can contribute to and help shape society. But is new construction always the best solution to the supposed problem? Sometimes, as client or designer, it may be necessary to question this assumption. Facing the enormous additions expected to cities worldwide, questioning a project's initial objectives—among a palette of options like using less material, reusing material, and repurposing material— is a powerful option and is sometimes the best solution.

A project by French architects Lacaton & Vassal illustrates the value of doing everything with nothing, albeit certainly in a different way than R. Buckminster Fuller originally imagined. Asked as part of a brief to embellish an existing square in Bordeaux, they studied how it already functions and determined that change was unnecessary. "Embellishment has no place here. Quality, charm, life exist. The square is already beautiful. As a project, we have proposed doing mostly nothing, besides some simple and quick maintenance work—replacing the gravel, cleaning the square more often, treating the lime trees, slightly modifying the traffic—to improve the square's use and satisfy the community's needs."[2]

1 Attributed to Rem Koolhaas, circa 2005.

2 See http://lacatonvassal.com.

# Propositions 23–37

## 23
## Share Functions

Collective use / shared spaces: design and build collective spaces whenever possible to reduce building volume (and material use)! Share functions—such as washing in collective laundry rooms!

## 24
## Increase Waste Costs

Make waste disposal super expensive in order to create a case for business and industry to recycle and reuse!

## 25
## Act Collectively

Learn by doing and sharing!

## 26
## Create Value

If it has value, it is collected (recycled); if it doesn't have value, create value. Unlock hidden values through research and systems thinking!

## 27
## Change

Help change "culture"!

# 28
# Localize

It's the (local) economy, stupid! (Sorry, Bill Clinton.) The global economic structure is based on politics and corporations. But it is the local economy that bears the cost of waste management and the failures of federal policy. We must document the cost of doing nothing—the cost of the environmental, social, and economic impacts of climate change. Doing something will cost less over the long term.

Learn from your locality!

Local culture matters! Re-materializing construction is linked and must be understood through the local scope. Each pebble is important and necessary in developing a global sustainable culture. As intangible ingredients, each is a clue to articulating local culture, local economy, and local social and environmental awareness. Incorporate local decision-making in the global sustainable agenda!

# 29
# Let Scarcity Be Your Inspiration

Start with yourself:
– Do you need a car?
– Do you need the size of your apartment?
– Do you have to fly?
– ...

# 30
# Communicate ... Disseminate

Spread the word! Inform, inspire, and empower the public—beyond expert circles.

# 31
# Avoid Doing the Wrong Thing

"A man has not everything to do, but something; and because he cannot do everything, it is not necessary that he should do something wrong."
Henry David Thoreau,
*Civil Disobedience*

## 32
## Maximize Usage

Make the most of it: maximize building usage! For example, facilities that are used by a school during the week can be opened to the community for the rest of the time. Organize various types of activities within them to maximize financial efficiency but also community cohesion! Don't build more buildings; bring more operators/activities into fewer buildings!

## 33
## Increase Awareness

Let the owner know—increase awareness! We need to increase public awareness concerning how many resources buildings consume.

## 34
## Learn

Learn critically from the past, teach rooted in the present, educate aspirationally for the future!

## 35
## Voice Your Opinion

"It takes a great deal of bravery to stand up to our enemies, but just as much to our friends."
Albus Dumbledore /
J. K. Rowling

Be critical and honest about all aspects of new construction materials promoted by investors, developers, and contractors! Many new companies are marketing bio-based materials as being sustainable without sharing their full data sets. Bio-based materials are not necessarily sustainable. There is need of awareness and open knowledge.

# 36
# Design for Time

We live in a world of perpetual change, and yet we design our buildings as if they will never change. The "life" of an entire building is hardly considered beyond some code and minimum-specification requirements. Very little consideration has been given to being able to replace or recover our materials over time, or to matching durability to length of use. The research of Stewart Brand and his 1994 book *How Buildings Learn* show us how buildings are continually tearing themselves apart because of the different rates of change of the various components and layers. His diagram of the "shearing layers of change" should be in our minds when we design and construct our buildings to allow for change over time and to allow for replacement and recovery of materials and systems.

# 37
# Regenerate Natural Processes

Regenerate processes of environments that can no longer support the scale to which humanity has grown. Nature is no longer an environment for a planet already radically changed by man. There are only natural processes.

Propositions 23–37

The additional propositions were submitted by the following participants of the LafargeHolcim Forum for Sustainable Construction held at the American University in Cairo in 2019:

Angelo Bucci (Proposition 31)
Diane Van Buren (Proposition 28)
Fernando Diez (Proposition 37)
Maria Gavozdea (Propositions 28, 32)
Heba Allah Essam E. Khalil
(Propositions 26, 28)
Yask Kulshreshtha (Proposition 35)
Marcos Mazari (Proposition 28)
Magda Mostafa (Proposition 34)
Michael Scharpf (Proposition 29)
Lloyd Scott (Propositions 25, 27)
Stuart Smith (Proposition 36)
Stefanie Weidner (Proposition 33)
Clemens Woegerbauer
(Proposition 24)
Anonymous (Proposition 30)

# Talks
# on
# Materials

# Make
# Do

Anne Lacaton

Make do with the existing, with people, nature, climate, the economy, in order to reinvent, to do more with less.

Making do is about using what we already have. It is about considering the existing as a valuable resource, not as unsatisfactory or constraining.

Each existing situation is an opportunity consisting of elements, qualities, and capacities that can be integrated,

On the site for a holiday house in
Cap Ferret was a sand dune with almost
fifty pine trees. The house was designed
in such a way that both the trees and the
dune could be conserved.

The location on top of the dune allows
for sweeping views. The trees growing
through the living room blur the
boundary between inside and outside.

60

reactivated, and reused. Each existing structure offers materials that can drastically reduce the need for new materials. Each site permits invention and imagination.

It is necessary to observe an existing structure from within in order to reveal its qualities and how to use what is already there, instead of systematically replacing and remaking. Today, the existing is the new material. It is always more sustainable to add onto, join, expand, and span what already exists than to empty a site and start over. The existing is the basis and the material, or rather the found material, of the majority of our projects at Lacaton & Vassal.

Make do with nature.

In 1998, we were asked to build a holiday house in Cap Ferret in the southwest of

France. We first looked at the location carefully. It was an exceptional and fragile place—a sand dune with almost fifty pine trees among the vegetation. We decided not to cut down any trees and to build the house as lightweight as possible in order to not change the dune. We used a simple and standard steel construction with elements that could be easily brought on-site and a foundation that did not require excavation or damaging the ground. The house was built four meters aboveground and accommodates the trees. From inside looking out, the construction disappears, giving place to the landscape and foliage.

> Making do with the existing is an opportunity to make a more sustainable master plan—that is, another way of making the city.

Saint-Nazaire in the west of France held a competition to build 300 separate houses.

The starting point for the design of a housing project in Saint-Nazaire was the question of how to preserve as much as possible of the forest found on the building site.

Instead of the 300 separate buildings the competition brief asked for, the architects proposed a three-story building on pilotis with walkways to access the apartments.

The intervention on the ground is kept
to a minimum. The lightweight structure
is raised twelve meters aboveground
on pilotis, allowing the forest to grow
beneath.

As we inspected the site, we were struck by the wonderful forest that was being continually diminished by development. So instead, we proposed to build a collective housing unit with a lightweight structure twelve meters aboveground in order to give the forest a chance to recuperate and continue growing. The simple construction also freed up the ground for public use.

> Make do with the climate to benefit from natural resources, save energy, and provide a better quality of life.

Our practice has learned a lot from agriculture, greenhouses especially. These intelligent constructions efficiently manage the climate, using a minimum amount of materials to capture the warmth of the sun and provide natural light, natural ventilation, and simple shading techniques. Greenhouses led us to develop the design of the double-envelope construction, which saves energy while also creating pleasant climatic conditions and extra space.

> Make do with abandoned buildings to reuse, to give life again, to invent use.

In 2013, we participated in a competition to turn an old industrial building in the French city of Dunkerque into a contemporary art center. The building stood alone in a shipyard that had been demolished in the 1980s. We were fascinated by the void within the building and felt that it would be a mistake to fill this wonderful space with floors, to isolate it and install air conditioning, which would radically change the building. We proposed saving the void and building a twin building right next to the existing building. The empty space of the existing building would remain unaltered and could be used for exhibitions or other public events, while the new building offered the structural

conditions required for the art center.
The double envelope of the new building is
very thermically efficient and provides extra
space on the top of the structure, allowing
for a view of the surrounding landscape,
the harbor, and the seaside.

> Make do with a minimum of materials
> to provide more space for use, to
> spend better and less.

For an architecture school in Nantes,
we wanted to provide as much space as
possible for the students and school to use
as they liked. Our intention was to use the
least amount of materials possible. The
materials make up around 8 percent of the
entire volume of the building; 92 percent
of the volume can be given to the space
and its use.

We think it is important to use only the
material necessary and nothing more. The

An old boat warehouse was to be transformed into a center for contemporary art.

The building was one of the last remnants of a shipyard that had been demolished in the 1980s.

Instead of dividing the space with floors and smaller gallery spaces, the architects proposed to keep the entire volume of the big hall.

To accomodate all the spaces the client asked for, a second building was created that duplicated the volume of the existing one.

city of Bordeaux asked us to propose a project to embellish a square in the city. We carefully observed the square twice a week over a period of four months, and our feeling was that it already had quality. The proposal we delivered to the city was to do nothing.

> Make do with housing blocks to transform, reuse, upgrade, to extend life, to give more with less.

We conducted a study of large modernist housing developments from the 1960s and 1970s. At the time they were built, these structures held an optimistic, utopic vision: a modern way of living that was affordable to everyone. But today these buildings are mostly neglected and viewed with disenchantment. In the mid-2000s, a national project of urban renovation was launched in France to demolish and rebuild almost 200,000 of these flats,

The project maximizes the usable
space with a minimum of materials.
Large unprogrammed outdoor and
indoor spaces can be appropriated
by the students.

which required relocating their inhabitants. Faced with this project, we teamed up with the architect Frédéric Druot to study the situation carefully. In 2004 we released our report, entitled *Plus*, which was based on the opposite approach to demolition: transformation.

In France, between 2006 and 2015 125,000 dwellings were demolished and 100,000 rebuilt—a loss of 25,000 units. The cost of the demolition and reconstruction of one dwelling amounted to 165,000 euros. Our alternative approach showed that it is possible to significantly transform a dwelling for the cost of 55,000 euros. Our approach is never to demolish, subtract, or replace, but always to add, transform, utilize, extend, give more to do better. We studied these modernist housing developments from the inhabitants' point of view, considering the basic qualities that every dwelling should have. Our goal

was to transform each dwelling to give it
the same qualities as a villa—a home that
is not just a box with narrow windows
but that can open up to provide a better
quality of life and a relation with the
outdoors.

Transformation means openness, extension,
more space, more light, more freedom
of use. In 2017, with Frédéric Druot and
Christophe Hutin we completed a project
of transforming a series of 1960s social-
housing blocks in Bordeaux. From the
outside, the buildings might be considered
ugly and without value; demolition had
been envisaged by the city. But from the
inside, one can see that these buildings
are made of individual situations, all of
them different. Every inhabitant in the
530 apartments gave personal value to the
interior space with their own decoration,
furniture, and plants. Our starting principle
was that the outside didn't matter; the

Three large social housing blocks from
the 1960s, intended to be demolished,
could be saved and transformed.

Where once there was only the exterior
wall with a small window, there is now a
large sliding door and a generous, light-
flooded winter garden.

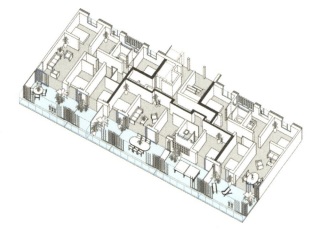

To keep the construction time as short as possible, winter gardens and balconies were delivered and installed as prefab elements.

Big openings for floor-to-ceiling sliding doors were cut into the old facade, and each apartment was enlarged by a three-meter-wide winter garden and a balcony (in blue).

transformation starts from the inside. That is, we will not change the quality of the existing structure, we will rather see what is missing and what can be improved without disturbing the lives of the inhabitants. So we proposed a four-meter extension on the south facade, which benefited each dwelling. This extension and the renovation of the interior could be realized without having to relocate the inhabitants—a construction process that is integral to the design. The extension is made with a double-facade system that allows it to be open during the summer and closed during the winter. The quality of life and pleasure of the interior space experienced by each inhabitant radically improve just by adding this extension, which moreover provides efficient insulation.

For this project, 100 percent of the existing structure was conserved. The usable surface of each apartment increased by an average of 50 square meters. Energy consumption dropped by 60 percent because of the insulation created by the winter gardens. Rent did not go up. The cost to demolish and rebuild was estimated to be 88 million euros, while the cost of the transformation was 35 million euros. Twenty percent of the financing was publicly subsidized from local and European partners, and 80 percent was subsidized by Aquitanis, the city's social housing office—14 percent by owner equity and 66 percent by bank credit. These numbers show that this transformation can also be done with a privately owned building.

We are currently collaborating with Frédéric Druot on a study of 1,600 sites of modernist collective housing in Paris to see what possibilities exist to improve and increase the housing stock and optimize

From the winter garden there is an expansive view over Bordeaux. The winter gardens are not heated and work as a thermal buffer.

The transformation was not only cheaper than demolishing and constructing a new building, it also used far less material, reduced the energy consumption of the building, gave the inhabitants more space, did not destroy the community, and turned something considered ugly into something beautiful.

the urban terrain. Our goal is to show that today we can continue building by fully using the capacity of the existing, without having to extend our cities.

Based on an inventory and detailed studies, we have identified 450,000 existing dwellings that can be transformed and see the potential to build 135,000 new dwellings on plots already built upon, equipped, and connected to public transport, which is extremely valuable for the city economically. But these projects require a big change in thinking about materials and planning methods. They require adopting a case-by-case strategy that looks at each site carefully to propose specific projects based on the given conditions—the opposite of a master plan.

# Sustainability Triad: Three Timber Buildings

Christine Binswanger

"Sustainable development is development that meets the needs of the present without compromising the ability of future generations to meet their own needs."
Gro Harlem Brundtland,
*Our Common Future*, 1987

The well-known triad of environment, economy, and society depicts the many dimensions of sustainability in an understandable yet complex way. Architects must plan buildings—and

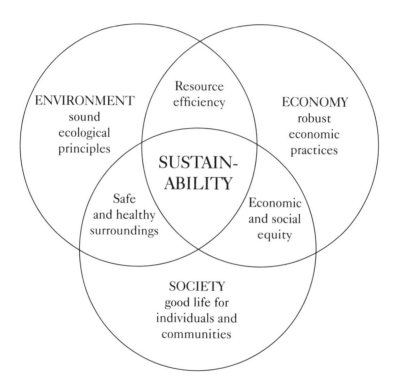

Environment
sound
ecological
principles

Resource
efficiency

ECONOMY
robust
economic
practices

SUSTAIN-
ABILITY

Safe
and healthy
surroundings

Economic
and social
equity

SOCIETY
good life for
individuals and
communities

Sustainability as a complex triad of
environment, economy, and society.

cities—where people feel comfortable, find their manifold needs satisfied, and treat others with respect. As its needs evolve, a community must be able to identify with, take care of, and reuse buildings and cities instead of tearing them down. How long does a structure need to last? How easily can it be repurposed?

> Economic and environmental efficiency is tied to a building's life span; the question of flexibility is essential in this respect.

The need to treat the environment with care is largely undisputed, yet the value of resource-saving planning is not as widely recognized. It is only with the help of specialists that we can measure the actual resource consumption of what we plan, which will lead us to develop new approaches.

Herzog & de Meuron has used wood as a central material in large public buildings in regions where it is readily available. Wood is a renewable material. It is easy to assemble and disassemble, and, when sourced locally, requires little energy for transportation. It is a material whose use maintains and expands local craftsmanship and know-how, from traditional methods to contemporary computer-aided technology.

> Since most people find wood agreeable, buildings made out of wood tend to be better cared for.

Owing to easy prefabrication, building with wood is a fast process. Unfortunately, however, the price of timber is too high—a carbon tax on construction materials would help make wood more competitive on the market.

In the second half of the twentieth century, the Swiss valley of Toggenburg was a well-frequented family resort. Left off the usual Swiss tourist routes, its popularity declined in the early twenty-first century. The infrastructure that brought people up the mountains had not seen major investments or renovations for half a century and neither had the hotels and restaurants, and because of climate change the area was not receiving as much snow as it once had. Thus, for the resort to survive economically, it needed to shift its focus from being a winter ski resort to a year-round destination. It had to attract a broader clientele and reinvent itself based on its own culture and qualities. Instead of trying to compete with the Swiss mega resorts, it had to offer a different kind of program.

The pioneer for this shift in values was the summit restaurant in the cable-car station on the Chäserrugg peak.

Located in a protected area, the project, constructed between 2013 and 2015, was closely observed by natural conservation agencies—a circumstance that impacted the choice of materials and building methods. Except for the crane, which was transported by helicopter, all of the construction equipment and materials were transported by the cable car in the course of its regular operation. A concrete factory was installed on-site that used local stone as the aggregate for the extension of the building's concrete base. Timber from the region was used as much as possible. Local craftspeople worked on the structure, the interior fit-out, and the majority of the furniture.

The building is rooted in the community, and it helped the cable-car business stay profitable. The construction method led to the cable-car staff identifying with the project, and they would explain the

Existing cable-car station with restaurant, originally built in 1972, on the summit of Chäserrugg, 2262 meters above sea level.

The concrete slab of the terrace stands out from the mountain and the sloping roof shape follows the incline of the surroundings. The building cantilevers over the narrow ridge on which it stands.

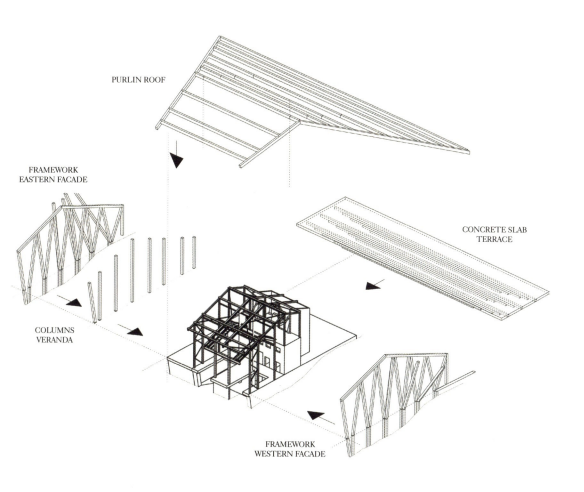

PURLIN ROOF

FRAMEWORK
EASTERN FACADE

COLUMNS
VERANDA

CONCRETE SLAB
TERRACE

FRAMEWORK
WESTERN FACADE

Structural additions to the existing
building.

Ascent to the new summit station.
The large roof connects new and existing
elements.

87

During events, the restaurant terrace turns into seating for the audience.

The sofa area and fireplace inside the restaurant.

construction process to the visitors during the ride up the mountain. There are many regular local visitors to the restaurant year round, which is also due to the fact that the building was constructed by local craftspeople. Local carpenters have even gained additional business by selling furniture to visitors who order pieces they see in the space. We believe the use of wood contributes to this overall success. Of course, the fabulous surroundings, cuisine, friendliness of the staff, and flexibility for organizing events are also important factors.

Located in a natural setting at the edge of the city, the Children's Hospital Zurich is a horizontal three-story pavilion-like structure. Fourteen courtyards provide daylight and orientation throughout the building. The patients' rooms—the most private zones—are fully wooden prefabricated structures on the top floor. Each room has its own roof.

The project's design has been given the top ranking in the Swiss Sustainable Building Council's rigorous evaluation system. Planning began in 2014 after the project won an international competition in 2012, and completion is scheduled for 2022. Timber is the predominant material of the facade. Concrete appears in specially handcrafted details, such as cavities in which wooden bars rest or concrete spheres underneath timber posts that keep them dry. The depth of the facade and perpendicular wooden "lattice" walls create privacy, especially for the treatment rooms on the ground floor. The timber elements include supports for plants that grow on the facade.

The use of wood, combined with the low scale of the building, the integration of nature and daylight, and the craftsmanship of the details, creates a memorable healing environment that lets children feel at ease (owing to the scale) and piques their curiosity (through the details and materials).

These "soft factors" of the architecture are also of particular interest to parents, who play a major role in their children's health and recuperation, and the hospital employees, who work better in a pleasant environment. Attracting and retaining the best talents is a challenge for any hospital. Aside from the substantial use of wood, the hospital is built to be as flexible as possible in the planning phase and use of the buidling—which might sound paradoxical since a hospital is a highly defined functional organism.

Concrete elements are reduced to columns, slabs, elevator shafts, and stairs—the minimum amount of the material needed to carry and stiffen

The depth of the facade and the perpendicular wooden lattice walls create privacy for the treatment rooms on the ground floor. On the upper floor, each patient's room has its own roof.

The load-bearing structure is primarily concrete, while the patients' rooms and facade are made of timber.

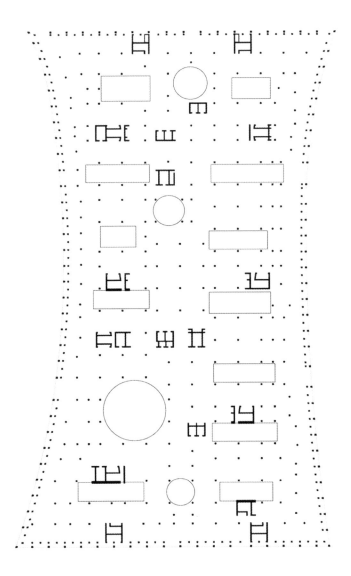

With the building's main elements in concrete (columns, elevators, vertical distribution), the structure allows for flexibility, which was a demand of the client's, both during planning and once the building is in use.

the building. Everything else is a lightweight construction in drywall or wood, easy to transform and dismantle.

Wood is featured prominently in the Vancouver Art Gallery project, a multilevel public building in a North American urban context. The material relates the art museum to the history of the city, which was built primarily out of timber until the 1950s. Over the last few decades, wood was largely abandoned as a construction material as downtown Vancouver developed its commercial districts predominantly out of glass. The use of wood in this project makes the gallery feel approachable and non-institutional.

The ground floor consists of a wooden structure that houses two free-of-charge galleries, a library, a café, and a shop. This low structure also frames a public

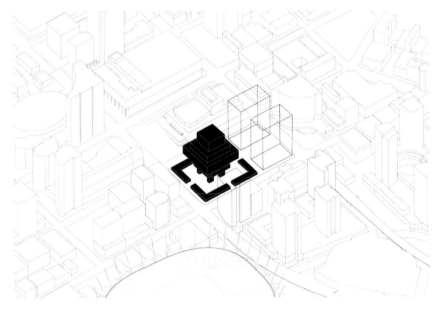

In 1912, Larwill Park appears as an
empty area surrounded by a dense
fabric of three-story wooden buildings.
Today, it is one of the last open spaces in
downtown Vancouver. The site's historical
use ranged from parade grounds to a
place for political demonstrations to a
hub for cultural and sports events.

Permeable low buildings line the block
and enclose an intimate public courtyard.

The enclosed, protected courtyard is a contrast to the surrounding busy, traffic-heavy streetscapes. Wooden finishes add to an overall warm and soft feeling.

Glass is used for most weather-exposed parts of the facade. Wood is used on the ground floor—the large "teeth" or "pillows" on the underside of the recessed terraces—and for the areas of the skin that are better protected against rain.

courtyard. About one third of the galleries are laid out in the first underground level around two sunken gardens, while the majority of the galleries is in the tower that rises above the courtyard. From the tower, visitors can look over the city to the ocean and mountains beyond—a typical Vancouver view. Elevating this mass frees up the public space underneath, letting in sun from the sides while providing shelter during rainy periods.

The pragmatic composite structure of the museum is made of concrete, steel, wood, and glass. Utilizing wood—an underused local, renewable material—helps promote its use for larger structures. The museum welcomes people into the space by offering a human scale among the glass towers of downtown, and it relates to the specificities of the climate by providing shade from the sun and protection from rain.

The project addresses the need for a public institution to provide space for everybody, not just gallery visitors.

It is located on a piece of land that is the only remaining undeveloped block in downtown Vancouver. Over the centuries, this area of the city has been a place for the community in many different ways, from parades and political demonstrations to cultural and sports events. The Vancouver Art Gallery, having been offered this valuable piece of land, gives the city back to itself, transformed.

# Place – Nature – Energy – Recycling – Materiality

Lord Norman Foster

To speak about the materials of construction, as a designer, is to take into account the context of the materials. Starting with history: it's been said that if you want to look far into the future, first look far into the past. History is inseparable from place. Sustainability, similarly, is inseparable from nature. Ever since I began designing, I've felt that a building would be healthier if it incorporated fresh air and if it related to the sun, to the landscape—this has now been scientifically proven. Sustainability is inseparable from energy, its consumption and harvesting. In an ideal economy, whether that of a city or a building, sustainability is also inseparable from the process of recycling—which leads us back to materials. As a designer, I may want to dematerialize the material, I may want it to evaporate, to disappear, or I may want it to have solidity. These themes—history, nature, energy, recycling, materiality—weave through my design practice.

> In my first meeting with Steve Jobs about the Apple headquarters in Cupertino, he talked about how Silicon Valley was the fruit bowl of America in his youth.

We talked about the possibility of re-creating that landscape, not as the setting for a building, but as the project itself. The challenge of Apple Park was to transform a site of around seventy hectares that has twenty-four buildings and is mostly covered in tarmac into a green landscape and creative environment for twelve thousand people.

The building is shaped like a ring and has a diameter of a half kilometer. The view from above is very different from the reality on the ground. When you're in the space of the circle, it's very much about the landscape; the building almost evaporates into the background. The building creates an inner sanctum, the social heart of the community, while appearing to those on the ground as an incident in the landscape. One hundred percent of the twenty-four buildings that occupied the site was recycled into the concrete for the foundation of the building. The 10,000 trees planted absorb

The idea of Apple Park was not only to build headquarters but also to re-create a landscape. When inside the circle, the building almost evaporates into the background.

around two hundred tons of carbon dioxide annually. Everything remained on-site so nothing would go into a landfill. The construction was about doing more with less. Concrete, which is inherently basic, was polished like marble, a noble material.

> When I first started my design practice, I felt that views and ventilations were of utmost importance.

This was scientifically demonstrated in 2016 by the Harvard School of Public Health. A study found that performance in a test environment simulating a super-green building was markedly higher than in a conventional or even a green building. The theme of working with nature, the breathing building, also recurs in a very different context: the Bloomberg Headquarters in the middle of the historical center of London. The building's facades, bronze set in stone, are its gills. Half of them filter the air and filter out the noise, contributing to the interior environment and reducing the energy load. In most temperate climates, expensive cooling and heating are not needed 70 percent of the time.

The materials of the building were determined by the historical city context. To be a good neighbor to the seventeenth-century Christopher Wren church and the Magistrates' Court, local stone was chosen for the material. The very form of the Bloomberg building, which is cut through with an internal arcade, is again a response to history. On an old map, Watling Street, the original Roman road, can be seen running through the building site. The new development took away the earlier buildings on the site, and, with the arcade, re-created the line of Watling Street.

> If we examine the building internally—its materiality, how it functions—we can see the way it breathes, the natural light, and the movement of pedestrians spiraling up toward the light.

The ecology of the building, its sustainability, is embedded in its circulation route. The floor of the workspaces is wood, which in an office environment is unusual because it tends to create echoes and reverberations. But the ceiling, made out of two and a half million petals, works as an acoustic counterbalance. One in five petals has an LED light source. The ceiling goes hot or cold according to the weather conditions, so the air modifies the climate of the building in a very holistic approach. The

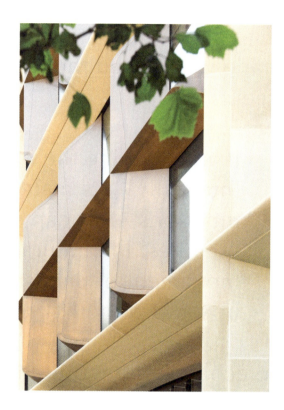

The building's facades are made from bronze and stone. Fifty percent of them also filter the incoming air.

The building adapts to the historical context by using local stone.

A multifunctional ceiling made from two and a half million petals; one in five has an LED light source and each works acoustically. It also heats or cools the building according to the weather conditions.

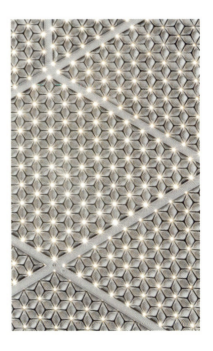

building also uses the aircraft technology of a vacuum system that uses virtually no water. Rainwater and gray water from the building are collected and recirculated by vacuum flush toilets. With a BREEAM rating of 98.3, it is the most sustainable building of its kind developed so far.

> Around ten years ago, in Abu Dhabi, my firm was involved in a project called Masdar. It was a series of experiments to demonstrate the feasibility of a totally solar-powered community for several thousand people and a university devoted to the study of renewable energy.

Twenty-four hours a day, seven days a week, Masdar is completely powered by a ten-megawatt solar field that only uses 40 percent of the energy it generates. Here, once again, similar themes arise:

How do you learn from history?
How do you learn from a civilization
that was able to create agreeable
environments externally and
internally in an age before you could
flip a switch for plentiful cheap
energy? How do you work with
nature?

In this typical desert city, the heat,
around 66°C, is modified by the way
the streets create shade and are scaled
to the individual—which taught us that
in Masdar, the motor vehicle should
be below pedestrian level. In these
cities, traditionally, courtyards with
vegetation create a cooler microclimate,
and the inner sanctum of the home is a
comfortable 27°C. By contrast, the felt
temperature in the center of Abu Dhabi,
with its tarmac and typical Western
response to a specific climate, can reach
71°C. Learning from history, the center

The ten-megawatt solar field powering Masdar produces about twice as much energy as the new city consumes.

The perforated screens of the facades provide sun protection, while their shape and ornamentation refer to the local context.

Like in old cities in a desert climate, Masdar has small shady streets and courtyards with vegetation to create a cooler microclimate. With this approach, the temperature in the center of Masdar can be reduced to 33°C.

of Masdar is a comfortable 33°C—less than half the felt temperature in the surrounding city. The residential units for the students use desert sand as an aggregate for the building's outer layer. Behind the outer layer is a deliberate gap to allow the movement of air, and then there is a layer of recycled aluminum. In this experiment, the university building learns from space technology, whose challenge is to create extraordinarily high levels of insulation against intense heat, much hotter than in the desert, that is both lightweight and high-performance.

> How do we transition from dirty carbon production to cleaner forms of energy? Cities are not only the present reality, they are the future.

By 2050, 68 percent of the world's population is predicted to be urban.

One in three individuals will live in an informal settlement without access to clean water, modern sanitation, or power—or all three. Cities consume 70 percent of energy worldwide, but they also generate extraordinary wealth. Mobility, automation, robotics, electrification, and clean energy will need to change. Why, for instance, should agriculture stay in the countryside, where it's removed from its ultimate market and where water is scarce, when urban farming might be done with far less water, transforming the city of the future into a green city? How will London look in 2050? Will offices still command the same kind of space, or will they become urban farms? And what in turn would happen to the countryside if it is consumed by vast networks of highways?

Thinking globally and acting locally, how do you recycle a village?

In Graubünden, in the Swiss Alps, there is a village of 800 people called La Punt-Chamues-ch. Last year forty young people left — 5 percent of the population — to move to cities. The challenge here is to create a center that would bring in people from tech industries in cities like Zurich, London, or Tel Aviv to create a third kind of visitor, a working visitor attracted to the lifestyle that this area offers. The inspiration for the project is first the architecture of the local villages from a time before cheap energy, which used insulating, protective windows, recessed and painted white, to pull in more light through small openings. The second inspiration is the landscape, and the third, the remarkable Swiss artist Matthias Becher. His paintings are a combination of the local architecture and the mountains.

Learning from history and also trying to fit sympathetically into a historical

La Punt-Chamues-ch, a rural community
in the Swiss Alps, wants to attract young
people from the tech industry.

Design inspirations: traditional windows recessed in deep walls and painted white to pull in more light through the small openings, and paintings by Swiss artist Matthias Becher that combine the local architecture and the mountains.

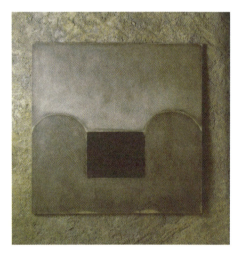

Mountain-like volumes made from local
material create a protective perimeter.

A large indoor space is the equivalent of
a village square within the building.

environment, we tried to create a kind of overcoat, or perimeter, that would be protective while also generating spaces within, and whose volumes would be echoed externally, mountain-like, using local materials. The taller volumes are the working spaces and the larger indoor space is the equivalent of a village square within the building. It is a kind of a village within a village where the working visitors and the local community interact.

This building was developed from another one located about a twenty-minute-drive from La Punt. This residential building is a combination of prefabricated high-tech elements and the local tradition of building with shingles. Individual pieces of hand-cut larch, around a quarter million in total, were applied with a high-tech device to the exterior. This is my family's

The facade of this residential building in Switzerland is made from local larch shingles. It was completed twenty years ago and won't require any maintenance for the next hundred years.

home in Graubünden, which was created twenty years ago. The local larch—recyclable, sustainable—looks as fresh as ever today, and will lead a maintenance-free life for at least the next hundred years.

# Harvesting Materials in a World of Finite Resources

Laila Iskandar

A global discourse on materials must address the issue of the harvesting and repurposing of waste. Traditional waste management systems in the Global South are embedded in realities that are often too complex for systems based on the European model to understand. These informal, socially constructed systems are difficult for city planners to accommodate because they developed from the needs and realities of urban inhabitants and were not determined or implemented on a governmental level. They derive from the residents' knowledge of informal markets and trading systems and provide the most destitute segments of society with incomes, livelihoods, trades, occupations, and economic growth opportunities that other sectors do not provide. The waste collectors turn the city's refuse into daily earnings so that they can care for their families, whom the state has left lacking in education and social services and for whom there are few prospects for improvement. Since they are not properly supported by the city, even though they achieve higher recycling rates and generate employment for significantly larger numbers of people than the official systems, the collectors end up adopting unsanitary and unsafe methods.[1]

The system of informal waste collection in Cairo began in the late

1940s. The *waahis* ("people of the oases") performed this daily door-to-door service, repurposing paper waste to sell as fuel to food vendors and the public baths.

They established a system of trash-collection routes among themselves. The waahis eventually began contracting the work to migrants from southern Egypt who had come to Cairo because of severe drought and religious friction in their villages. According to these informal work arrangements, the waahis hired the new migrants to collect trash on their routes, and these collectors would give the waahis the paper waste as payment and keep the rest, which primarily consisted of organic waste that they would feed to the pigs they raised in the city. The waahis acted as labor contractors, and the *zabbaleen* ("trash collectors") did the regular and tedious work of door-to-door collection,

A *zabbaleen* (trash collector) on his
daily door-to-door route picking up
waste in Cairo.

A zabbaleen truck doing daily
door-to-door collection.

Zabbaleen recovering and processing
paper and cardboard waste to be resold
before ultimately going to a paper
remanufacturing plant.

thus keeping the city clean. The history of the waahis and zabbaleen is specific to Cairo, but it resembles similar historical arrangements in other parts of the world— an ethnic minority, in this case Coptic Christian, already excluded, finds low-skill work in informal arrangements.

In 1984, Cairo and neighboring Giza created new regulatory bodies—the Cleansing and Beautification Authorities— to formalize and upgrade the region's waste sector by documenting the collectors and banning the donkey carts used daily by the zabbaleen to transport the collected waste. The new authorities licensed the zabbaleen by delineating their collection routes, charging them a fee to collect waste from households, and allowing them to charge households a monthly fee for collection, which they'd have to split with the waahis for the contract work. The money the zabbaleen had left over scarcely covered the costs of operating and maintaining their vehicles, not to mention health and safety costs or other incidental expenses associated with providing their service.

> Their lack of education and information led them to miscalculate revenues and profits. The cleanliness of cities had become intertwined with a context of poverty: a lack of the capability of the waste collectors to negotiate and participate in the workings of the system.

The waahis' agreement with the zabbaleen had been that they could keep whatever waste they wanted except for the paper waste. However, the value of paper had drastically diminished by this point; the public baths had shut down and the number of street food vendors was dwindling. Waste had grown to include

The zabbaleen recycle 80 percent of the collected refuse. Here, plastic waste is sorted by color and then washed before being further processed.

glass, aluminum, tin, fabric, and so forth, which were harvested and repurposed by the zabbaleen alongside the organic waste. By signing a contract with the new regulatory authorities, the waahis were were able to maintain their level of earnings despite the devaluation of paper, and the zabbaleen still relied on the waahis to give them access to the waste and materials.

As the cleansing authorities were being established, the development agency Oxfam brought trash disposal machines to Cairo, setting up plants in the southeastern area of Mokattam where the zabbaleen lived. This sparked an industrial revolution. The agency provided the zabbaleen credit to purchase the machines and install them in their homes so they could valorize the materials and not just collect, sort, and sell the waste. The trash collected in Cairo was now brought to Mokattam to be sorted and sold to neighbors for processing. The compacted, granulated, washed, and pelletized waste was then sold to the manufacturing industry. These zabbaleen began their own export industry, selling granulated and washed raw materials to China, but this channel was cut off when new laws put an end to the export of PET plastic.

In the late 1990s, the city responded to the need to expand waste collection and processing to the whole of Cairo and end its dependence on dealing with organic waste by feeding it to pigs.

Composting plants were established that were expected to absorb a substantial amount of the city's waste and replace the unseemly methods of the zabbaleen, namely pig breeding. However, the plants and facilities were poorly managed, poorly

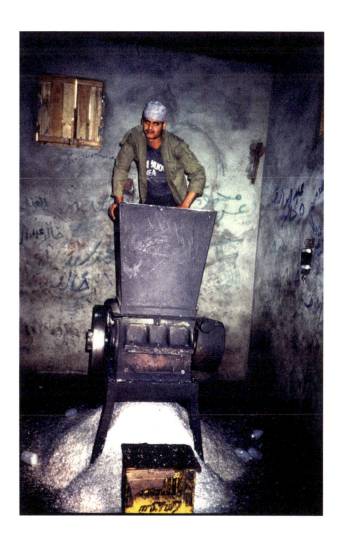

The zabbaleen collect and sort the
refuse and then process the materials
with machines purchased with a loan
from Oxfam. Here, plastic waste gets
crushed into pellets that are later sold to
manufacturers.

operated, and poorly maintained, and thus they weren't able to replace the service provided by the pig farming.

In 2000, the population of Cairo reached twelve million and was generating 10,000 tons of waste per day.

> The zabbaleen were collecting between 30 and 40 percent of this daily waste and recycling 80 percent of what they collected.

Local Egyptian companies were contracted to collect the waste in the neighborhoods not serviced by the zabbaleen and transport it to poorly managed municipal dumpsites. These sites became sources of billowing smoke that hung over the city of Cairo, which, together with the burning of rice straw in the delta region, created a suffocating atmosphere for at least two months of the year.

In 2003, the governorates of Cairo and Giza decided to unburden themselves of waste management by privatizing it. Contracts were signed with European multinational companies that had track records of keeping cities clean in Europe. The terms included waste collection from containers placed on the streets, ending door-to-door collection by the zabbaleen, and the transportation of waste to transfer stations and composting plants.

> Only 20 percent of the waste was required to be recycled (compared with the 80 percent managed by the zabbaleen), and the rest was to be dumped in sanitary, engineered landfills. A fee for this new collection service was automatically added to each resident's electricity bill.

This system, however, neglected to factor in the socioeconomic reality of the city.

The official data agency of the Egyptian government estimates that almost 33 percent of the country's population lives below the poverty line.[2] These inhabitants constitute a potential pool of scavengers, and informal markets can provide sources of income from the recyclables scavenged from waste pooling sites.

The multinationals could not attract the labor they required; the stigma attached to the occupation of trash collector acted as a barrier to unemployed youths joining their collection crews. The new trash containers placed on the streets were stolen at an alarming rate. Owing to the failure of the privatized collection system, a parallel system sprang up among high-income residents of the city that maintained the door-to-door collection by the zabbaleen. The residents gave them an amount they felt was fair while still paying the added fee on their electricity bills even though they were no longer receiving that service. Municipal agencies responded to the unsatisfactory condition of the streets by implementing a rigorous monitoring of waste contracts. They frequently fined the multinationals for violations not always related to their contracts, and the fines often exceeded the amounts owed to the companies. This situation led many companies to stop their service and go into arbitration, eventually resulting in a breach of contract.

In 2009, when the outbreak of the H1N1 flu became known by the misnomer "swine flu," the Egyptian government decided to take precautionary measures to protect the city from the possible outbreak of an epidemic.

They hastily embarked on culling the pig population in the country, starting in the neighborhoods of the zabbaleen since most pigs were raised there, and then extending to the rest of the country. The culling was criticized by the World Health Organization since the relationship between pigs and the H1N1 flu was denied by all authoritative international agencies. However, the official waste managers had made their decision, which left the city without its main organic-waste recyclers and further penalized the zabbaleen by taking away a significant part of their livelihood. The city was soon swimming in a sea of organic waste that the zabbaleen had no incentive to collect. To make matters worse, the pig culling ended right before the month of Ramadan, when food consumption and rates of organic-waste generation rise. All of this coincided with the strikes of the multinationals. The situation reached unsanitary levels the city hadn't experienced in years.

Municipal waste managers must carefully consider replacing functioning traditional systems with seemingly modern and efficient ones. In Cairo, policies need to be implemented that empower the zabbaleen economically and providing them with sanitary and environmentally friendly conditions.

In 2015, a waste-management regulatory authority was established to develop a new framework to counteract the mistakes of the privatization model.

It is supposed to integrate the informal sector, support municipalities in contracting waste collection, and map the facilities. New policies need to work with existing informal networks to develop municipal infrastructure that attempts to be sustainable and equitable, even if it does not follow conventional Eurocentric models of urbanism.

1 See Plastic Technology Center, *National Study Plastic Recycling Sector*, Industrial Modernization Centre – Egypt, January 2008, http://www.imc-egypt.org/index.php/en/studies/finish/121-full-study/93-plastic-recycling-development-strategy; and CID Consulting, *The Informal Sector in Waste Recycling in Egypt*, report submitted to GTZ, May 2008, http://www.middleeastpdx.org/resources/wp-content/uploads/2013/03/THE-INFORMAL-SECTOR-IN-WASTE-RECYCLING-IN-EGYPT2.pdf.

2 Central Agency for Public Mobilization and Statistics, *Income, Expenditure and Consumption Survey, 2017–2018*, Cairo, 2019.

The Talks on Materials are adapted from keynote speeches at the 6th International LafargeHolcim Forum for Sustainable Construction, American University of Cairo, April 4–6, 2019.

# Changing Paradigms: Materials for a World Not Yet Built

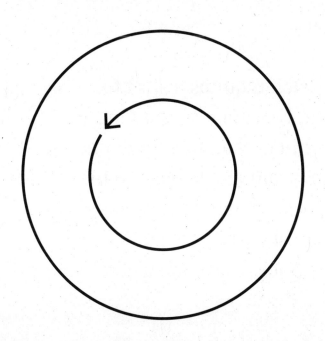

As the global population continues to grow and prosperity spreads, our environment faces intense pressure. Under our current model of construction, we extract resources from the earth and use them in buildings for a few decades, or perhaps centuries. Then the buildings are razed and the materials are discarded—we consume them rather than borrow them from nature. For a truly sustainable built environment, we must create a circular economy in which reused and recycled materials from today's building stock serve as the mines of the future.

This approach requires a shift to cultivating, breeding, or growing resources rather than merely extracting them—to minimize damage to the nonhuman environment. At the same time, we must consider water and energy supplies, waste management,

and alternative construction methods
that, while transforming our relation to
resources, also respect the human values
of dignity, health, and happiness.

Werner Sobek
Dirk Hebel

# Build More with Less: How to Create the Future without Destroying the World

Werner Sobek

Is the idea of building more with less a utopia? Maybe. But to me, it's the key to our future and a challenge we must urgently address. We must all tackle the social, economic, and environmental problems created by population growth, migration, climate change, and dwindling supplies of resources. How do we do this? By building differently and by reforming a construction industry that is famously resistant to change while creating a built environment that requires significantly less material.

To put this into a global perspective, note that in Germany the built environment accounts for an average of 490 tons of material per citizen, then note that the world population is growing by 2.6 people per second. Supplying every new person with Germany's structural standard would require extracting, processing, and installing almost 1,300 tons of building materials per second. The carbon cost is huge: creating a built environment similar to Germany's for all those newborns would result in a dramatic failure to meet the 2°C target agreed on in Paris—without taking into account $CO_2$ emissions from other sectors such as transport and manufacturing.

This means it's time to act. Neither today nor in 2050 will every person on earth be able to enjoy Germany's current structural standard. If, however, we allow today's inequalities to continue or even worsen, we face the prospect of far-reaching social destabilization. It is obvious that only a drastic reduction in material consumption and greater recycling will lead to a new type of construction.

At the same time, we must ask what level of consumption is appropriate. The construction industry accounts for about 35 percent of global energy use, 35 percent of emissions, 60 percent of resource consumption, and half of mass waste. These proportions add up to almost incomprehensible numbers when translated into absolute values, but they vividly illustrate the burden shouldered by the construction sector. The answer to the question of how the construction industry should contribute to solving the challenges we face could be described under the heading: *natura mensura* rather than *homo mensura*. Nature, not man, is the measure of all things. Under this principle, further objectives could be sketched out as follows:

1. It's about building for more people with less material.
2. It's about planning for the recycling of all building materials.
3. It's about an immediate halt to all emissions of gaseous waste.

"Saving energy" is deliberately absent from this list because humanity has no shortage of energy. Our problem is that our energy comes from burning fossil fuels, which produces emissions that contribute significantly to global warming. The sun provides us with 10,000 times as much power as humanity needs for everything we do. If we had focused enough of our intellectual effort on energy production from solar radiation or gravity, we could have eliminated $CO_2$ emissions from carbon-based fuels long ago. Sustainability, therefore, does not necessarily mean greater energy efficiency; it means a shift away from fossil fuels.

When discussing energy efficiency in recent decades, planners, building owners, and politicians have mostly focused on thermal insulation. This isn't bad, but it's not the only solution—and because insulation typically consists of synthetic materials, it often produces tons of hazardous waste when buildings are demolished. Furthermore, when legislators prescribe construction methods (a particular level or type of insulation) rather than the achievement of a goal (reducing the use of fossil fuels) they hinder new ways of thinking. Building codes that require walls, windows, roofs, and so forth, to have specific insulating properties limit our ability to develop alternative solutions in materials, construction techniques, or systems that are more sustainable. Rather than mandating specific methods or technologies, politicians should drastically reduce and ultimately ban the use of fossil fuels in the construction and operation of our buildings, which would allow us to solve our $CO_2$ problems without stifling innovation.

Minimizing our consumption of building materials makes sense not only because it would cut emissions of $CO_2$ and other gases. Simply meeting growing demand for buildings and infrastructure requires that we drastically reduce the amount of material we consume. Even increased use of renewable materials such as wood can't entirely solve the problems we face. In addition to minimizing the resources we use for construction, we must also make these resources available for later reuse. That means designing for disassembly, which can reduce the volume of new building materials that must be extracted while minimizing the amount of waste that can't be recycled or reused.

The changes needed to make construction sustainable are manifold and far-reaching. There are plenty of approaches, but society must be willing to implement them. We need a change in awareness, and we must create a legal framework that will allow it to happen. The market alone cannot and will not fix it. The market isn't oriented toward any collective goal, so it lacks both morality and conscience. Society itself needs to know what it wants, and legislators must implement this will. At the same time, politicians must stop prescribing methods to be applied instead of objectives to be achieved. How architects and engineers meet the goals developed by society as a whole should be left to their innovative power. Experts in their fields must have the freedom to develop the best tools and methods to address the problems we face.

# Cultivated Building Materials: The Fourth Industrial Revolution?

Dirk Hebel, Felix Heisel

The field of sustainable construction requires a holistic approach. Sociocultural, economic, ecological, functional, and aesthetic factors are considered and understood as equivalent and interacting with one another. This complexity prohibits simplified prescriptions and responses or general applications. Rather, sustainable construction strives to develop an unbiased, critical view and, as a result, an attitude toward the task based on basic knowledge and one's own experimental actions.

Therefore, the twenty-first century needs to face a radical paradigm shift in how we produce materials for the construction of our habitat. While the first industrial revolution resulted in a conversion from regenerative (agrarian) to non-regenerative material sources (mines), our era may experience the reverse: a shift toward cultivating, breeding, raising, farming, or growing future resources that goes hand in hand with a reorientation of biological production methods and goals.

Addressing the industrialization of building materials, it is obvious that the term "industrialization" describes different periods in history. The first industrial revolution, which began in the eighteenth century and reached its climax in the nineteenth century, was based on the invention of the steam engine to mechanize production. Starting at the end of the nineteenth century, the second industrial revolution is described by the use of electrical power engines to initiate mass production. The third industrial revolution took place in the middle of the twentieth century and used digital information technology to automate production. A fourth industrial revolution could be just ahead of us, reintroducing biological aspects into an otherwise mechanized, industrialized world. In the words of Klaus Schwab, founder and executive chairman of the World Economic Forum, this would be "characterized by a fusion of technologies that is blurring the lines between the physical, digital, and biological spheres."[1]

While the mechanized world that has emerged since the first industrial revolution aims to establish an endlessly reproducible state of "exactly the same," any biological process resembles a unique process in itself, allowing an endless variety of "almost the same." The digital can be seen as an in-between state. Leaving—at least for a while—the physical dimension of a possible product behind and, for example, calculating or mimicking a growth process with its expected variations in order to find the best circumstances can help generate and cultivate particular adaptive qualities. In this way, the digital realm can be used to plan the sourcing of the best growing conditions from available data pools without undergoing a time-consuming trial-and-error process. Here, a new understanding of a bio-mechanized or bio-industrial production is required, one which allows for a higher degree of deviations and abnormalities.

For this to be operational, any shift toward a new order in the industrialization of building materials must respect, adapt, and further develop the established frameworks of norms, regulations, and standards concerning health, safety, and durability. The concept of industrialized building with nature does not promote a move backward to the preindustrial age; it seeks to describe ways to progress within the given industrial setting in order to modify and reinvent it. This also applies to the social conditions of production and the cultural acceptance of new materials and construction methods. The introduction of biologically driven and digitally supported production processes could allow so-called late-comer economies in less industrialized areas of our planet to participate in this revolution.

A similar thought was formulated by Thorstein Veblen in his 1919 thesis, in which he addressed Germany and Japan as latecomers to global industrialism.[2] From this perspective, latecomers have the potential advantage of using the knowledge and advancements of more developed nations—without having to go through the same (painful) period of growth. "This privilege encompasses all technological and organizational innovations. The challenge, obviously, is to identify the good in both the new and the existing and blend them with a minimum negative consequence."[3] Cultivated building materials, considered in the

Mycelium hyphae form a dense matrix that can be activated as natural glue in biological composite materials and fulfills the criteria of the fourth industrial revolution.

The MycoTree at the Seoul Biennale of Architecture and Urbanism in 2017 was the first structural application of mycelium-bound building elements.

context of a possible fourth industrial revolution, could provide a promising new economic, ecological, social, and cultural order—which, this time, might emerge from regions in the Global South, adding a new chapter to the history of industrial production with protagonists as ingenious and far-reaching as those of the nineteenth and twentieth centuries.

Some of the organic matter that could be turned into building materials is at present seen as unwanted or labeled repulsive. For example, while the pharmaceutical

Newly developed structural building elements from mycelium-bound agrarian waste materials.

industry uses bacteria with undisputed success, architecture and construction have not yet activated and exploited such capacities. The same is true for mushroom mycelium. Mycelium hyphae form a dense matrix that can be activated as natural glue in biological composite materials and fulfills the criteria of the fourth industrial revolution.

Bamboo, another material that has been used for centuries as a reliable resource for construction, has never advanced to the level of an industrialized construction product, as if locked in a box labeled "vernacular." High-rise scaffolding structures in Hong Kong, traditional buildings in Southeast Asia and Japan, or highly individual signature architecture, like a number of buildings by Simón Vélez, Jörg Stamm, Kengo Kuma or Vo Trong Nghia, all come to mind. As a cultivated building material, the potential of bamboo lies not only in the application of the raw material but also in its extremely strong fiber. The extraction and reconfiguration of bamboo fibers has the potential to prompt the building industry to develop new industrialized production methods.

For this reason, biologists, bioengineers, ecologists, chemists, and material scientists need to collaborate with architects and civil engineers to foster a broader understanding of how to approach the complex task of cultivating our future building materials. Supplemented by economists, this multidisciplinary work

has the potential to hone our conception of alternative urban models in which production constitutes an integral part of a future urban society, calling for new types of spaces and infrastructures.

This text is an extract from the introduction of Dirk E. Hebel and Felix Heisel, *Cultivated Building Materials* (Basel: Birkhäuser, 2017).

1 Klaus Schwab, *The Fourth Industrial Revolution* (New York: Random House, 2017). The four evolution steps of a so-called industrial revolution are inspired by this publication.
2 Thorstein Veblen, *The Place of Science in Modern Civilisation and Other Essays* (New York: B. W. Huebsch, 1919).
3 Zegeye Cherenet Mamo, *Designing the Informal: Spatial Design Strategies for the Emerging Urbanization around Water Bodies in Ethiopia* (Hamburg: Hafen City University, 2015), 208; see also Dirk Hebel, "Materializing Informality," in *Lessons of Informality: Architecture and Urban Planning for Emerging Territories; Concepts from Ethiopia*, ed. Felix Heisel and Bisrat Kifle (Basel: Birkhäuser, 2016), 166–70.

Through varying production parameters, mycelium-bound composite materials can also be grown as high density and performance boards for the construction industry.

# Mushroom Materials Named under the Sun

Phil Ross

The sun rains its wealth of light upon the earth as it has for many billions of years. A highly efficient carpet of photosynthetic trees and plants weaves this energy into structured material reserves of lignin, cellulose, and other sugars. The accumulated wealth bound within these organic materials is released and dispersed as they are consumed by other organisms. For a long time people have benefited from plants and animals as a way to increase material production, and now mushrooms are being harnessed as an engine for more efficient and less polluting forms of manufacturing. With this knowledge one thing is certain: the future is rotten!

For the most part, mushrooms live as a colony of interwoven threadlike cells. They thrive by decomposing and consuming dead plants; the mesh-like body of the mushroom breaks down plant material and then rearranges it in plastic configurations and chemical organizations within its own networked body. This transformation takes place on both the micro and the macro scale, making mushrooms well suited to process the huge volumes of organic waste produced each year from agriculture, forestry, and farming.

Mushroom materials were first developed as an artistic medium to grow temporary sculptural forms. The process of growing mushrooms is not unlike making bread; it is a type of fermentation, the same process used to transform sugars into alcohol and milk into yogurt. The primary technology that drives commercial fermentation is pasteurization, the practice of steam-

Reishi mushroom in
the forest, 2009.

Piles of sawdust
destined for growth.
Far West Fungi,
Monterey, CA.

SEM image of
Ganoderma mycelium.

*Kind Recognition*,
2000. Ganoderma
mycelium substrate.

Detail of mycelium brick experiment, 2009. Ganoderma mycelium substrate.

*Yamanaka McQueen*, 2013. Ganoderma mycelium substrate, oak salvage wood, carriage bolts, beeswax, tree resin.

Fine mycelium leather, 2016.

*Mycotecture Experiments
(Salt & Pepper / King & Queen)*, 2011.
Ganoderma mycelium substrate.

cooking materials as a way to neutralize foods so they do not get infected. These ideas are well established and practiced globally with agreed-upon standards and measures. But it was soon discovered that materials grown from the dense living matrix of a mushroom could be used to make advanced composites, foams, and performance plastics. These materials can be grown into the texture of urethane foams with surfaces that are velvety and fluffy, leathery and rubbery, or beetle-shell brittle and shiny. In addition to this, consumer products grown through a process of fermentation and decomposition require far less energy, water, and other resources than conventional manufacturing.

MycoWorks was formed in 2013 with the aim of using this technology to develop materials that could replace the petroleum-based composites used in furniture and home construction. Although there was great interest from consumers and designers, it was unclear how to increase the scale of manufacturing to achieve competitive prices with existing materials. Within our current economic system, polystyrene and other plastics used in furniture and home construction are as cheap as can be and will continue to be used until something better—or new regulation—comes along. Petroleum and its derivatives are also underwritten by huge investments, so it was unrealistic to expect a start-up to have any competitive advantage in these

Detail of mushroom composite for fine machining, 2014. Ganoderma mycelium composite.

markets. This meant the biggest obstacles were not due to technology, efficiency, or performance, but had more to do with the paths toward investment and the legal frameworks to promote the use of alternatives.

This realization led to a reconfiguration of MycoWorks, which looked at where materials were valued at a premium. The problem and the solution were found in the world of fashion, where there is both a consumer and a market demand for alternatives to the animal skins and plastics used to make apparel. By molding the body of the mushroom into a sheet and processing it in many of the same ways as animal leather, a sensual and strong material for luxury fashion was developed.

Market demand for mushroom materials has been driven by concern about the stability of future global supply chains. Consumer demand, however, arose from ideological realizations and, in particular, a shift in thinking that seeks to effect political change through purchasing decisions. The lesson of minimizing waste is heard by those struggling for a continued existence ten years into the future. So it seems that efficiency is not the only attractive aspect of these kinds of materials, but so is their plastic ability to conform to the problems at hand.

The ability to grow synthetic wood, open cell foams, and leather analogs is only a small demonstration of what this technology is capable of. Our knowledge of mushrooms is fractured between different industries, areas of expertise, and histories of study; in this new field of applied materials, there is an urgent need for basic measurements and standardized physical parameters at the microscopic level. If we are to fully understand this emerging area of husbandry, it's going to require significant investment—as well as smart people focused on thinking about rotten things. Only through a new language of physics and genomics will this world become apparent and we can call these materials by their true names.

# Reuse and Recycling: Materializing a Circular Construction

Felix Heisel

Ever since the industrial revolution, the global economic system has been based on a single linear pattern: the "take–make–throw" model. Companies manufacture products using harvested or extracted materials and consequently sell them to consumers who—once the products are broken, old, or out of fashion—dispose of them, including all their embedded raw materials, water, energy, and knowledge. As a result, global material extraction has more than doubled in the past thirty years.[1] And it is predicted to continue on a similar path, from 65 billion metric tonnes of raw materials entering the economic system in 2010 to around 82 billion in 2020.[2]

To break this pattern, there must be a paradigm shift in the underlying approach, one that will radically change our economic and ecological understanding and decouple economic growth and resource consumption: a shift from a linear to a circular economy.

This transition offers potential material savings worth more than one trillion dollars.[3] Within the circular economy, material resources are used continuously in either biological or technical metabolisms at their highest value and utility, without ever turning into waste. In combination with new business models that separate performance and hardware, this allows manufacturers to retain ownership of their resources, leading to an increased security in stock management for production. Most importantly, the circular economy is not an end-of-pipe solution but a new economic model with a design imperative: when the product itself

Linear Economy

Take – Make – Throw
Energy from finite sources

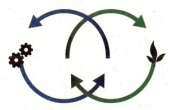

Circular  Economy

Take – Make – Repeat
Energy from regenerative sources

# The paradigm shift:
# From linear to circular economy.

is the raw material for the next creation, it makes sense to design for disassembly into pure-type raw-material cycles; and when companies only sell services and lease products, it makes sense to design products that are compatible, long lasting, and easy to repair.[4]

The concept of cycles thus plays a fundamental role. In general, the smaller the loop the more efficient it is in terms of energy and resource input.[5] This is commonly understood through the three $R$s — reduce, reuse, and recycle — which were extended into a legally binding European hierarchy of waste management operations: (1) prevention, (2) preparing for reuse, (3) recycling, (4) other recovery, and (5) disposal.[6] Interestingly, reduce and reuse are now almost hidden within the category

of prevention, which technically is not even a waste-management operation, as both quantitative and qualitative waste prevention concern substances or objects before they become waste. The same is true for direct reuse of valued substances or products.

Once an element has been declared waste, it is however mandatory to fulfill one of the waste-treatment steps in order to achieve a so-called end-of-waste status through material recovery (2, 3), or less ideally incineration (4) or landfill disposal (5).[7] Today's reported recovery rates often include high percentages of operations that do not fulfill the criteria above of closed material cycles within a circular economy, where materials, components, and products should be kept at their highest utility and value at all times. In terms of the waste hierarchy, only preparing for reuse at that moment satisfies these criteria, while recycling would need to exclude all downcycling processes. Other recovery and disposal represent economic, ecological, and sociocultural losses and should be prevented. Ideally, with respect to the sought-after paradigm shift, materials, components, or products should never fall into the scope of waste legislation.

All materials
in the unit are fully
reusable, recyclable,
or compostable.

Various concepts, such as design for disassembly,[8] product as service,[9] or extended producer liability,[10] aim to prevent the intention, need, or interest in discarding substances or objects by ensuring their utility and value within a closed-loop application. The result would be a city that is restorative and regenerative by design, where materials circulate in endless cycles from one use phase and application to the next through reuse or high-quality recycling. Yet the construction of cities for deconstruction in the form of a material depot has hardly begun. To test the viability of the circular concept, in 2018 Werner Sobek, Dirk E. Hebel, and I built a full-scale experiment at the Swiss Federal Laboratories for Materials Science and Technology (Empa) NEST research building in Dübendorf.

The Urban Mining and Recycling (UMAR) unit is underpinned by the concept that all the resources required

The Urban Mining and
Recycling Unit at the
Empa NEST building.

The Mehr.WERT.-Pavillon's structure uses sixty-year-old undocumented steel from a former coal power plant.

to construct a building must be fully reusable, recyclable, or compostable. In its investigation, UMAR addresses a wide range of scales and topics, such as alternative building materials, circular construction methods, urban material

cadastres, and new economic business models. The unit's supporting structure and large parts of the facade consist of untreated timber; the portal frame of the facade is covered in repurposed copper sheets from the roof of an Austrian hotel. The interior of the unit contains an extremely diverse range of serially manufactured building products, whose various constituent materials can be separated and sorted before being introduced back into their respective materials cycles. Among the technologies used are cultivated mycelium boards, recycled bricks, repurposed insulation materials, and reused door levers. The greatest innovation lies in the connections, which can all be easily reversed because materials are tucked, folded, or screwed rather than glued. Consequently, pure type-sorted recycling or pure biological composting of all elements is feasible at the end of the unit's use time.

Most building legislation makes no distinction between material use cycles. For example, in Germany reused or recycled products or materials must comply with the standards of DIN or EN norms with respect to structural, fire, health, or other specifications—like any virgin resource. This is both an opportunity and a limitation: On the one hand, if a material's certification exists, there is no reason to not use reused or recycled resources. The problem is that most of the time no such certification exists for reused elements. Missing documentation about origin as well as treatment during use phases makes this step particularly difficult.

The Mehr.WERT.Pavillon by KIT Karlsruhe and the office 2hs, located on the premises of the 2019 Federal Garden Show in Heilbronn, aims to prove that the urban mine provides high-quality material resources for structural applications. Next to recycled glass, plastics, and mineral demolition waste, the pavilion's structure is made from reused steel that was reclaimed from a disused coal power plant near Dortmund. In addition to a detailed visual inspection to determine possible damage to the elements, the steel was tested at KIT laboratories for tensile strength, elasticity, notched bar impact strength, and chemical composition—enabling the reuse of this sixty-year-old steel in a structural application. This example clearly demonstrates the feasibility of circular construction, and it also highlights the important steps that still need to be made in terms of material quality, selection, and documentation.

1  "Global Material Extraction by Material Category, 1980–2013," *materialflows.net*, http://www.materialflows.net/materialflowsnet/trends/analyses-1980-2013/global-material-extraction-by-material-category-1980-2013/ (accessed January 7, 2018).
2  Ellen MacArthur Foundation, *Towards the Circular Economy 1: Economic and Business Rationale for an Accelerated Transition* (Cowes, Isle of Wight: Ellen MacArthur Foundation, 2012).
3  Peter Lacy and Jacob Rutqvist, *Waste to Wealth* (New York: Palgrave Macmillan, 2015).
4  Ellen MacArthur Foundation, *Towards the Circular Economy: Business Rationale for an Accelerated Transition* (London: Ellen MacArthur Foundation, 2015).
5  Walter R. Stahel, "Product-Life Factor," paper presented at "The Future and the Private Sector," The Woodlands, TX, 1982.
6  European Parliament and the Council, *On Waste and Repealing Certain Directives 2008/98/EC* (Brussels: European Parliament and the Council, 2008).
7  European Commission, *Guidance on the Interpretation of Key Provisions of Directive 2008/98/EC on Waste* (Brussels, 2012).
8  Felix Heisel, Dirk E. Hebel, and Werner Sobek, "Resource-Respectful Construction: The Case of the Urban Mining and Recycling unit (UMAR)," lecture at "SBE19 Brussels IOP Conference Series: Earth and Environmental Science," Brussels, February 5–7, 2019.
9  Walter R. Stahel, *The Performance Economy*, 2nd ed. (London: Palgrave Macmillan, 2010).
10 Walter R. Stahel, *Circular Economy for Beginners* (Geneva: Product-Life Institute, 2018).

# Reuse Economy

Maarten Gielen

Rotor is a cooperative based in Brussels that aims to redesign the material economy of the city. We work toward a condition where repeated reuse of materials and components is the norm. With this in mind, we draft policy proposals and analyses but also conceive and realize interiors and buildings. In 2011 we set up Rotor Deconstruction, a contractor specialized in salvaging and reselling building components.

Rotor redistributes hundreds of tons of reclaimed materials per year and is considered a pioneer in this field. We work in collaboration with dozens of other companies through a network of salvage operators that we established. Opalis currently regroups around 140 companies, mostly in Belgium, but efforts are underway to extend its reach to include France, the Netherlands, and the United Kingdom, and to increase the number of listed companies to 1,500. The idea is first to document the existing practices in order to form a basis for the further development of trade. Gradually, this platform will serve other purposes; Opalis has been used to share technical specification sheets for widely traded materials such as bricks and cobblestones, which helps inform future policy work.

The challenges in the field of architectural salvage are surprisingly simple. While the assumption is often that the bottlenecks to widespread reuse must be of a technical nature, this is not our experience. Technical issues do exist for a number of materials (i.e., how to remove cement mortar from ceramic tiles without breaking them), but public funders and research institutions stand in line to help tackle them.

Very often, however, technical solutions do not automatically translate into an ongoing process of salvage and reinstallation. Why is this? Reuse is almost always preferred over the option of applying newly produced materials when a reduction of greenhouse-gas emissions and the conservation of nonrenewable raw materials are at stake. Yet in Western Europe massive quantities of easily reusable materials — even those requiring virtually no treatment for reuse — go to waste each year. Take, for instance, the case of concrete pavers. Installed in a bed of sand without mortar, these pavers are nowhere near the end of their life span when they are replaced after a few decades, at best, of use. Typically, the existing pavers are downcycled into rubble, and newly cast pavers are installed.

Pavers in natural stone, on the other hand, are almost always reused. This can easily be explained: while the cost of salvaging both concrete and natural-stone pavers is the same (around €7 per m²), the spread with the price of new pavers in natural stone (minimum €50 per m²) is much higher than with new concrete pavers (minimum €16 per m²). New concrete pavers are simply too cheap for anyone to invest in the infrastructure needed to bring salvaged pavers to the market. Or, more precisely, labor costs are too high compared to the material cost.

What is true for concrete works for many of the energy-intensive materials used in contemporary construction: in mature economies they are too cheap. Externalities, such as the considerable carbon emissions from cement production, are not included.

In our current economy, individuals are taxed on their earnings to finance the needs of the community. The exploitation of common resources, on the other hand, is most often heavily subsidized. It would make more sense to invert this logic and enforce steep taxes on the exploitation of natural resources and the burden these concessions put on the global community (air, water and soil pollution, global warming, habitat destruction, etc.), while reducing taxes earned on labor. The result would be a world in which common sense would prevail: an economy where it is more reasonable to reuse concrete pavers than to see them end up as rubble.

Franck, located in Kampenhout, Belgium, started out in the demolition sector over forty years ago. The company now specializes in the recovery and resale of bricks, mainly salvaged from their own deconstruction works. These bricks are sorted, cleaned, and placed on pallets, a very labor-intensive job. The more common Flemish bricks are constantly in stock in large quantities, and smaller lots of rarer bricks are also offered.

Active for over forty years in Thirsk, North Yorkshire, Cleveland Steel & Tubes offers an extensive range of salvaged steel pipes and tubes for use in construction and infrastructure. The bulk of their steel originates from the oil and gas industry, where over-ordering or over-rolling has created a surplus in stock and supply. The company can offer product traceability and certification to varying levels and in line with individual client and project requirements.

The company Maris Natuursteen
specializes in the recovery of natural stones.
Their assortment includes natural stone such as
Swedish granite, sandstone, Belgian porphyry,
white sandstone, and Balegem stone. They have
a constant and impressive supply of the
so-called Napoleon heads, or Burgundian
cobblestones. Maris has the necessary machinery
for the transformation and processing of their
various stones.

For 35 years the family business Van Hameren
Houthandel, located in Ter Aar, the Netherlands,
has been active in the trade of reused wood.
In their stock, which spans three hectares, they
sell wood in a wide range of types, forms, and
sizes, from small apple boxes to mooring posts
of fifteen meters. The bulk of their stock
consists of wood sourced in the Netherlands.
Thanks to an extensive network of building
contractors, they can ensure a constant stock of
large lots of different wood types.

The stock of Jan van Ijken Oude
Bouwmaterialen resembles a true Valhalla of
prewar building materials. On their one-hectare
site in Zemnes, the Netherlands, they store
their supply so efficiently that almost every
conceivable interior element or old building
material is present in an enormous variety of
colors and formats. Jan van Ijken started
selling used tiles from northern France and
Belgium in the 1980s. Later, structural wood,
bricks, roof tiles, and stone floors were

added, to name but a few material categories. All goods are selected for their high aesthetic value and durability, and their range includes cast-iron radiators and forgings, wooden floors and parquet, antique doors and fireplaces, porcelain washbasins and industrial lighting, and natural-stone tablets and door handles.

# Paradigm Shift: The City of 1,000 Tanks, Chennai

"The Great Mother created the world in water. She makes the future in it. This is how she speaks to us."

> The Kogi people, Colombia

Imagine Earth without political boundaries. Imagine nature and humanity working in close collaboration. Imagine the planet's natural systems becoming the guiding structure for overlapping and interrelated political organization. One way to consider this vision is through the lens of water, an element that flows in an interconnected cycle: as water falls on Earth, cities, buildings, and people, it crosses boundaries and affects everything from crop yields to ground stability. Water is a vital resource for all life, yet it is also associated with many of the greatest threats to humanity, from melting ice caps to toxic rivers.

A holistic approach to water management can be an emblem for a culture of sustainability.

The way we live at the moment is an entirely different scenario. Cities have been designated places of consumption rather than part of the world ecology, even though they are dependent on natural processes. Because we (especially in the Global North) have sought protection from nature through architecture, we have become estranged from nature. The false dialectic of nature and society has allowed humans to extract water and materials from Earth for their own short-term benefit and immediate financial gain—a linear habit that does not consider "externalities" or waste. If nature is a factory, continually producing everything from rich alluvial soils to oxygen and clean water, then our

169

current modus operandi has been factory liquidation: selling whatever stock is on supply while throwing out the "machines" that can do the work. Nature is complex and therefore not easy to predict perfectly; hence, modern cities have preferred to rely on artificial systems whenever possible. This has gradually created the disasters we face today. But if humanity in the Anthropocene has the power to alter the world to such an extent that it no longer supports life, it should also have the power to restore nature to ensure its continued existence in a sustainable manner.

Existing paradigms need to be updated, and nature and natural processes must be holistically integrated into the very cities that have tried to keep them out for centuries. Nature, rather than posing multiple risks, provides multiple benefits: vegetation can not only turn sewage into clean water for reuse, it also prevents floods and erosion, sequesters carbon, cools and filters the air, and provides space for biodiversity. Putting nature back to work in resource production requires a different attitude: humanity will no longer "steal" (extract) water from Earth but rather "borrow" it. This means giving it back to the natural cycle of rainfall and evaporation in the same pure condition and amount in which we received it. By integrating nature into the urban realm, cities will be able to exist in harmony with the planet, not in opposition to it. In this new paradigm, there is no externality, there is no water debt for future generations—everything

is connected to planetary ecology and economy. This future scenario will not be built at once but will grow incrementally through small local projects tied to a large-scale collective and sustainable vision.

The economy is buoyed by artificially deflated transportation costs helped by cheap fossil fuels redistributing materials around the globe while creating disparity and volatility. This centralization of resource management and production has made the processes that support life invisible and immutable: water magically comes out of a tap and is flushed far away; the consumer has no comprehension or agency in the system. But an urban community that makes the reality of nature visible, collecting its own water, producing its own food and energy, and treating its own waste, is more likely to make rational, sustainable decisions than a community dependent on intangible networks. Stitching water systems into the urban fabric and overlaying them with multiple functions helps build local capacity, making these systems a tangible part of people's lives.

How a systemic and holistic approach to water management can be designed, financed, and implemented in a dense urban context is the subject of the City of 1,000 Tanks project in Chennai, a city with ten million inhabitants in the southern Indian state of Tamil Nadu. Centuries ago Chennai was a leading example of smart water

Water collection: Women in the Chitra Nagar public housing complex in Chennai can spend up to four hours a day collecting and transporting water from hand pumps to their homes.

Water tankers: As Chennai faces droughts caused by climate change, inhabitants become increasingly dependent on tankers that extract water from rural areas and sell it at high prices in urban areas where water is scarce. This creates imbalances and tensions within the region.

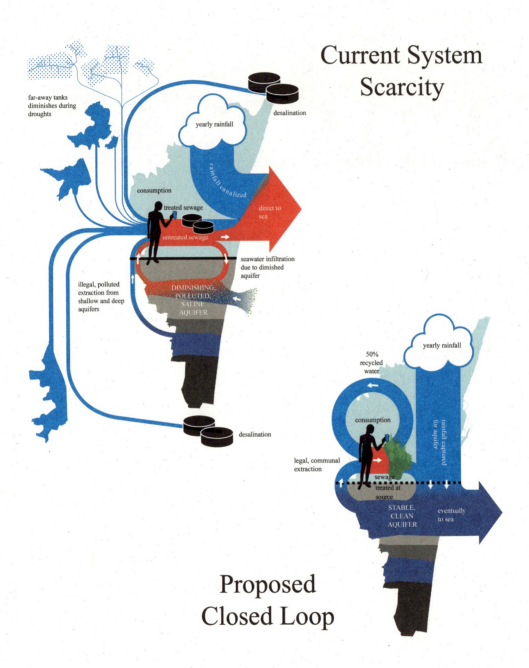

Current System
Scarcity

far-away tanks
diminishes during
droughts

desalination

yearly rainfall

consumption

rainfall canalized

treated sewage

direct to
sea

untreated sewage

seawater infiltration
due to dimished
aquifer

illegal, polluted
extraction from
shallow and deep
aquifers

DIMINISHING,
POLLUTED,
SALINE
AQUIFER

desalination

50%
recycled
water

yearly rainfall

consumption

rainfall captured
for aquifer

legal, communal
extraction

sewage
treated at
source

STABLE,
CLEAN
AQUIFER

eventually
to sea

Proposed
Closed Loop

172

Scarcity versus abundance: Chennai currently works with a perception of scarcity — water is transported across long distances from unsustainable sources to nourish the city. Chennai receives more than enough rain to supply its population, but the rainwater is quickly expelled into the sea. Wastewater is not reused as an asset, it is rather allowed to pollute the aquifer. By closing the water loop locally through rainwater harvesting and wastewater recycling, Chennai can become resilient.

management, demonstrating how urban communities could live in proximity to seasonal water hazards and still be in harmony with nature. Lakes, rivers, and temple tanks composed Chennai's ecosystem. These water bodies acted as occasional reservoirs, absorbing water in the monsoon season and replenishing ground reserves for later use in the dry season. The urban patterns around them were adapted to annual change. Local communities were responsible for management and maintenance.

The city is now developing along a different path. Technical solutions neglect tradition and natural conditions and tend to be shortsighted. Today, Chennai's peak seasonal rainfall is dumped into the ocean as quickly as possible through an extensive pipe system. Overwhelmed by the amount of rainfall and clogged by silt and sewage, these systems have failed to protect citizens from severe flooding. Half of the city's sewage is expelled into rivers and storm drains, polluting the shallow aquifers and making the water unsafe for consumption. The other half is pumped through nearly 3,000 kilometers of sewer mains, often uphill, with hundreds of unreliable pumps that often fail. Chennai's relatively flat topography makes the complex system impossible to efficiently manage.

With an increase in per capita water consumption, population density, and geographic expansion, Chennai has begun to invest in desalination plants and

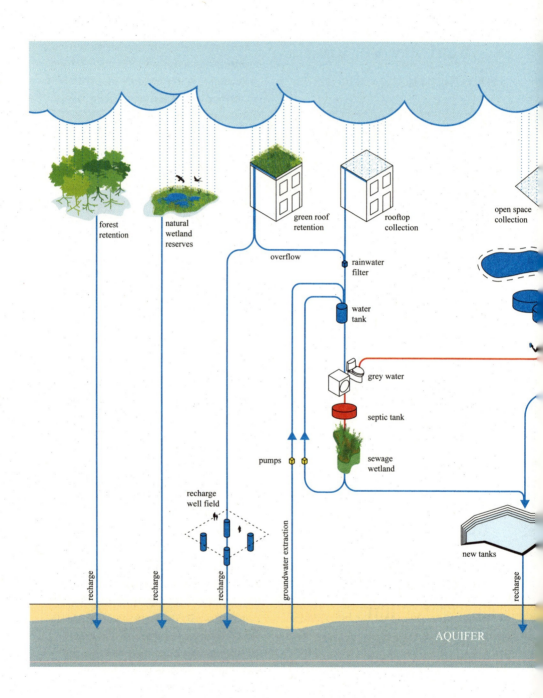

forest
retention

natural
wetland
reserves

green roof
retention

rooftop
collection

open space
collection

overflow

rainwater
filter

water
tank

grey water

septic tank

sewage
wetland

pumps

recharge
well field

groundwater extraction

new tanks

recharge

recharge

recharge

recharge

AQUIFER

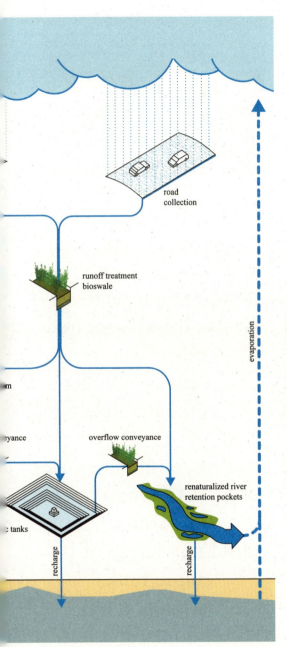

road
collection

runoff treatment
bioswale

m

yance

overflow conveyance

tanks

renaturalized river
retention pockets

recharge

recharge

evaporation

# Nature-based solutions collect and treat water and recharge the aquifer in a closed loop system.

distribution channels. Desalination triples or quadruples the cost of water production, uses vast amounts of energy, and negatively affects coastal environments. It exacerbates rather than solves the water problem by increasing the amount of wastewater that requires treatment. There is growing recognition that the sustainable management of groundwater resources is critical to mitigating the impacts of future climate shocks, significantly improving residents' resilience to drought, and serving as a buffer during dry periods.

The City of 1,000 Tanks offers a comprehensive "water balance" strategy for Chennai to adapt to drought and flood risks as well as prevent water pollution. The program intends to achieve water security by collecting rainwater, treating wastewater locally, and using both to recharge the underground aquifer for later extraction. This will be accomplished with plant-based low-cost technologies, so-called nature-based solutions that put nature to work in the collection, treatment, and storage of water. Measures such as constructed wetlands for sewage treatment, bioswales for runoff remediation, detention parks for stormwater absorption, and riverbank renaturalization can be integrated into existing neighborhoods to rejuvenate groundwater levels and solve problems locally. By establishing the right incentives and protocols to maintain these alternative green technologies, the City of 1,000 Tanks will cost half as much per volume of water compared to desalination. Additionally, the natural technologies proposed here "close the loop" by resolving water supply, flood prevention, and pollution all in one go. They also improve air quality, reduce temperatures, and enliven public spaces. If the city shifted to resilient water sourcing, it could save the equivalent of 850 million USD per year and avoid annual carbon emissions of three million metric tons.

To develop a solution for the entire metropolis, City of 1,000 Tanks starts with flagship projects. Working together with experts, government officials, vulnerable communities, and other stakeholders, the interdisciplinary team begins with a heritage project in Mylapore, a disaster-resilient housing project in Chitra Nagar, a green industrial project in Koyambedu, and canal restoration in Mambalam.[1] These projects will establish the necessary policies and connections between government departments and the private sector to implement a citywide water solution. Together, the projects can provide a water supply of 200 million liters per day, and if scaled up to the whole city, it could create a supply of up to 1,600 million liters per day.

Mylapore Temple Tanks: Mylapore was originally designed as a city with a resilient water infrastructure capable of retaining monsoon water for use in the dry season. Modern development patterns in this historic core of Chennai have erased the functionality and knowledge of its temple tanks. "Mylapore Trail" seeks to restore and enhance Chennai's water heritage, making it a proven model for the rest of the city as well as a sustainable tourist attraction. Two historic temple tanks that are not in use are to be restored in a collective effort to increase groundwater, which eventually will restore water levels in the tanks.

Chennai: City of 1,000 Tanks.

Mylapore Street during the dry and wet seasons: Public spaces are designed with nature-based solutions as new dynamic tanks that treat and store.

rainwater runoff, and private properties, both residential and commercial, treat and recharge gray water through decentralized nature-based solutions. An integrated network of bioswales connects the new tanks to make a resilient and highly visible system that increases awareness, highlights historic areas, and improves the overall attractiveness of the neighborhood for the benefit of tourism, commerce, and liveability.

Chitra Nagar Housing during the dry and wet seasons: The Chitra Nagar public housing development was badly hit by the 2015 floods, and the area routinely floods even with the slightest rainfall. Limited access to water, poor solid-waste management, and lack of sanitation facilities also burden the settlement. This housing scheme will be retrofitted to close the water loop through rainwater collection, recycling, and storage, along with solid-waste management, giving residents a reliable and clean source of water while preventing floods and standing water. The project has gained interest with the board in charge of the property as an innovative alternative to the redevelopment of the area and relocation of residents.

Mambalam Drain: Built on top of a former reservoir in the modern heart of Chennai, Mambalam, an important commercial center, faces both chronic flooding and water shortages. The canal that drains the watershed is neglected and choked with refuse and sewage.

Mambalam Canal during the dry and wet seasons: The City of 1,000 Tanks connects different socioeconomic groups through a common infrastructure to create resilience against climate change. The canal can be improved through visibility as a public space with constructed wetlands to clean influent sewage and retain excess stormwater.

1   The team is led by OOZE Architects in collaboration with Madras Terrace, IIT Madras, Care Earth Trust, Paperman Foundation, Biomatrix, Pitchandikulam Forest Consultants, the Rain Centre, IRCDUC, Urayugal Social Welfare Trust, Goethe-Institut, TU Delft, IHE Delft, HKV Consultants, and Professor T. Swaminathan. The team was selected by the Water as Leverage for Resilient Cities Asia, an initiative by the Special Envoy for International Water Affairs of the Kingdom of the Netherlands and the Netherlands Enterprise Agency (RVO) in close collaboration with the Greater Chennai Corporation (GCC) and 100 Resilient Cities (100RC). The initiative also partners with the Asian Infrastructure Investment Bank (AIIB), the Dutch Development Bank (FMO), the International Architecture Biennale Rotterdam (IABR), Architecture Workroom Brussels, the Global Center on Adaptation, and UN-Habitat, supported by the UN/World Bank High Level Panel on Water.

# Shifting the Flows, Pulling the Strings: Stocks, Flows, and Their Dynamics

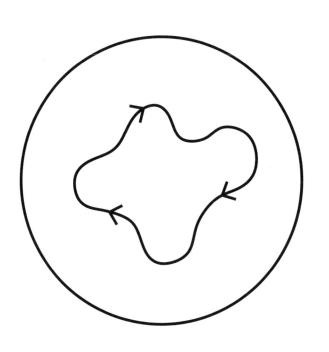

Would it be possible to think of the built environment as an opportunity to develop new solutions rather than as a problem that needs solving? How should buildings be reconsidered and cities organized to have a positive impact on both nature and society?

Construction can reduce greenhouse-gas emissions or even store carbon, but only if we make the right decisions throughout a structure's life cycle. In particular, this means paying attention to the materials used, as buildings can serve as temporary repositories of supplies to be mined later. A renovation, on the other hand, can become a catalyst for a reactivation of social and economic networks in a neighborhood. But harnessing these opportunities requires an intimate understanding of urban dynamics, as cities are complex systems that reflect the interactions between natural and human processes, so we need a combination of sociological, geographic, and mathematical approaches to support ecological restoration and reconnect the components of natural systems. In this section, we examine new ideas that promote a better future and assess how they can become part of our everyday routines.

Marilyne Andersen
Guillaume Habert

# Beyond Circularity

Marilyne Andersen, Guillaume Habert

Monitoring Material Flows
and Their Regenerative Values

In a world where data is ubiquitous, it might seem easy to monitor material and energy flows through urban systems. But, to quote the American environmentalist Donella Meadows, "we measure what we care about, and we care about what we measure."[1] Policymakers and society as a whole rarely acknowledge resource, energy, or water scarcity. More often than not, they are not properly measured, or only partially so, even though a misleading indicator can be as detrimental as no measure at all: both can steer us in the wrong direction.

There is no doubt that we urgently need to move toward a circular economy. In his book, Serge Salat argues that we should first think about efficiency on an urban scale, then move to a building-by-building approach to understand how people behave within the improved environment. This process can guide us away from the monofunctional urban model and help foster mixed-use and adaptability. On the other hand, Heba Allah Essam E. Khalil suggests we consider the city as a system, with inputs, outputs, and functions, and focus on monitoring resource flows. In urban contexts such as Cairo, this will be the only way to properly evaluate official ("formal") resource data against the actual ("informal") ones. That would allow us to better map flows and build on existing skills.

One of the most pressing challenges regarding data monitoring is to create demand. Much information considered valuable is already mined. What we lack is data about a city's hidden value. Access to data and platforms to make existing information more accessible are emerging but are still crucially needed.[2] In particular, although good practices tend to be more visible, publicizing failures can help deepen our understanding of the issues at hand.

Trigger Changes

The construction sector is typically conservative and risk averse, so simply showcasing alternative materials and technological solutions while explaining current societal threats won't be enough to induce change. Catastrophic events such as floods, fires, or earthquakes can create an incentive to reconsider how we build.[3] Architects, engineers, and scientists can then design for hope by implementing new solutions, some of which stem from traditional methods. In Mexico, for instance, rubble from earthquake was transformed into a wonderful cultural center.[4] And in South Africa, dignified houses have been built from waste left from clearing invasive plants.[5] But it can be difficult to initiate change in the absence of a dramatic event. New technologies such as the Internet of Things,[6] or sophisticated structural systems for high-rises,[7] have the potential to nudge clients toward new building types thanks to their

attractiveness compared to current standards, and thereby help in decreasing a structure's environmental footprint.

Circularity with
Social Quality in Mind

Urban quality can't be considered without integrating social concerns such as livability and diversity. While the twentieth century saw the rise of the suburbs, people today more often seek a high-quality urban lifestyle. The shift requires a combination of design, technology, and policy actions that promote circularity. Walkable environments and public spaces that nurture community building can be designed, but this depends on finding solutions to pressing questions ranging from land ownership to job and gender diversity, and from security and safety to tapping into the skills of residents and the cultural legacy of a place.

Shifting how we think about and work with resources can be a powerful tool in getting more people to engage. The city works as a system, and mapping its resources can prove particularly challenging. It also has untapped potential when scratching — literally — beneath the surface. For instance, studies show that accurate mapping of underground heat flows can be used to develop shallow geothermal infrastructure to keep residents warm,[8] or to build energy-efficient subterranean urban farms.

## Looking Ahead

There is a fundamental interdependence between the natural and the built environments. Unfortunately, as Christoph Küffer writes in his contribution to this book, most developments in the built environment actually worsen environmental and social conditions rather than improving them. While crises and emergencies can spur rapid change, traditional innovation cycles — starting with an idea, going through multiple tests, then prototypes and tests, and finally market release — are simply too slow. We need to support ecological restoration and reconnect the components of natural systems. New ideas that promote a better future are catalysts when they raise a question; they turn into an answer only when they become part of everyday life, embraced by the community, designers, and policymakers.

1 Donella Meadows, *Indicators and Information Systems for Sustainable Development: A Report to the Balaton Group* (Hartland Four Corners, VT: The Sustainability Institute, 1998).
2 See, for instance, https://metabolismofcities.org/.
3 Chrisna Du Plessis, "Chaos and Resilience," in *The EcoEdge: Urgent Design Challenges in Building Sustainable Cities*, ed. Esther Charlesworth and Rob Adams (London: Routledge, 2013).
4 Root studio, Juchitán (Oaxaca, Mexico), http://tallercapital.mx/.
5 Working for Water Program, Department of Environmental Affairs (DEA), South Africa.
6 M. Kamei, K. Kurisu, and K. Hanaki, "Evaluation of Long-Term Urban Transitions in a Megacity's Building Sector Based on Alternative Socioeconomic Pathways," *Sustainable Cities and Society* 47 (May 2019), article 101366.
7 S. Weidner, C. Kelleter, P. Sternberg, W. Haase, F. Geiger, T. Burghardt, C. Honold, J. Wagner, M. Boehm , M. Bischoff, O. Sawodny, and H. Binz, "The Implementation of Adaptive Elements into an Experimental High-Rise Building," *Steel Construction* 11, no. 2 (2018): 109–17.
8 Y. Zhang, K. Soga, and R. Choudhary, "Shallow Geothermal Energy Application with GSHPs at City Scale: Study on the City of Westminster," *Géotechnique Letters* 4 (2014): 125–31.

# How the Circular Economy Can Lead to Carbon Neutrality

Serge Salat

Over the next thirty years, the global urban population is projected to increase by 57 percent to 2.4 billion. Material consumption is predicted to grow even faster. Quantitative analysis of the global resource requirements of urbanization shows that without a new approach, material consumption by the world's cities will grow from forty billion tons in 2010 to about ninety billion tons by 2050, an increase of 125 percent. The high demand for raw materials far exceeds what the planet can sustainably provide. Resources must become a central policy concern—China, for example, used more cement between 2011 and 2013 than the United States used during the twentieth century. Producing its energy largely from fossil fuels, China has already become the largest carbon emitter in the world;

energy- and material-intensive urban development is regarded as the most significant driver of emissions.

The energy required for global infrastructure growth will play a critical role in accelerating climate change. As highlighted by the 2014 report by the Intergovernmental Panel on Climate Change: "The anticipated growth in urban population will require a massive build-up of urban infrastructure, which is a key driver of emissions across multiple sectors. [...] Currently, average per capita $CO_2$ emissions embodied in the infrastructure of industrialized countries is five times larger than those in developing countries."[1] International research has shown that the globalization of Western infrastructure using current technologies would correspond to about

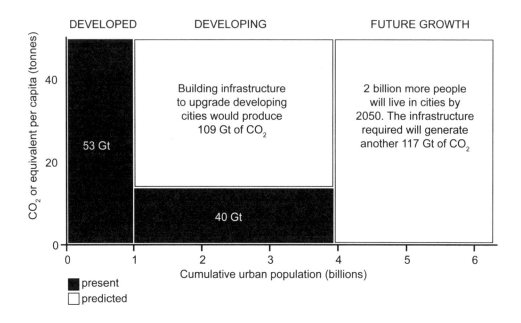

The urban development carbon challenge.

35 to 60 percent of the remaining carbon budget available until 2050 if the average temperature increase is limited to 2˚C, and thus may compromise that target.[2]

A promising opportunity for reducing carbon emissions in the built environment and infrastructure is incorporating the principles of the circular economy into all phases of a building's cycle, which can help meet the needs of the built space while contributing to the goal of carbon neutrality. The benefits include reducing the need for new construction, improving urban land use, reducing construction and operating costs, and increasing resource efficiency while strengthening the local economy.

Circular-economy approaches in buildings are needed to reduce the embodied emissions of the built environment. These include: designing buildings to be adaptable and easy to disassemble at the end of their life; using innovative products and technologies to make buildings more circular; designing buildings to be reused and refurbished instead of demolished; allowing maximum reuse of materials when deconstructing buildings; using innovative business models enabling more flexible use of existing and new buildings, and therefore more efficient performance; and planning sustainable infrastructure that can adapt over time. We need to define a hierarchy for building approaches that maximizes the use of existing materials with the aim of retaining existing buildings. When moving from "retain" to "recycle/compost," returns diminish: it is better to retain buildings than to reuse their materials after demolition. The hierarchy is supported by some key design principles: ensuring, through layered construction, that the different parts of the building are accessible and can be maintained and replaced; avoiding waste; designing for adaptability and dismantling; and selecting materials that can be reused and recycled.

A circular-economy approach in the built environment keeps buildings, products, and materials at their highest value for as long as possible. The pathway toward a circular economy requires spatial planning strategies to foster integrative flows of resources, including energy. In London, for example, the principles of the circular economy were incorporated into the draft plan for the regeneration project of the Old Oak and Park Royal development. The plan aims to create more than 25,500 new homes and 65,000 jobs on 640 hectares of residential and industrial areas while ensuring optimal circulation of local materials.[3] The main opportunity identified is the ability to reuse and disassemble

buildings and infrastructure. By capturing local resources such as water, heat, organic matter, and solid waste for reuse and allocating underutilized areas for agriculture, the plan aims to ensure the environmental and economic resilience of the area.

The scale and pace of transformation can be accelerated through the synergies created by circular-economy principles in the built environment: planning compact cities (dense, mixed use, transit-oriented); planning for local and circular material flows; designing for adaptable and flexible use; using collaborative design processes; integrating material choices into design; taking inspiration from nature; sourcing materials strategically; building with resource-efficient construction techniques; constructing "buildings as material banks"; maximizing the use of space through design features; using smart technology to run buildings efficiently; adapting buildings for alternative uses; and so forth.

Forward-looking cities are already accelerating the transition to a fully circular economy. London, Amsterdam, Barcelona, Copenhagen, Paris, and Phoenix have published road maps for circular economies and have begun to put in place the necessary policies, partnerships, and infrastructure. This approach will become crucial in the coming decades for all cities. The gradual reduction of waste through the creation

of alternative paths for material flows
is needed to safeguard cities' efforts
to reduce direct emissions in the case
of indirect emissions resulting from
increased consumption.

1  K. C. Seto, S. Dhakal, A. Bigio, et al., "Human
   Settlements, Infrastructure and Spatial Planning,"
   in *Climate Change 2014: Mitigation of Climate
   Change. Contribution of Working Group III to the
   Fifth Assessment Report of the Intergovernmental
   Panel on Climate Change*, ed. O. Edenhofer,
   R. Pichs-Madruga, Y. Sokona, et al. (Cambridge:
   Cambridge University Press, 2014), 927.
2  Daniel B. Müller, Gang Liu, Amund N. Løvik,
   et al., "Carbon Emissions of Infrastructure
   Development," *Environmental Science &
   Technology* 47, no. 20 (2013): 11739–46.
3  ARUP, OPDC, and LWARB, "Circular and
   Sharing Economy Scoping Study for Old Oak and
   Park Royal," Greater London Authority, April 20,
   2017, https://www.london.gov.uk/sites/default
   /files/9._circular_and_sharing_economy_study
   .pdf, 5.

# Enhancing Livability through Resource Efficiency: An Urban Metabolism Study in Cairo

Heba Allah Essam E. Khalil

Although cities are engines of economic development and concentrations of human activities, they are also hubs for consumption with the resulting environmental degradation.[1] Many experts call for decoupling resource intensity, economic development, and related urban development, especially within cities of the Global South, in favor of adopting a different path toward a green economy.[2] However, it is essential to highlight that urban development in the Global South is mostly attributed to informal urban growth. Such informalization necessitates a thorough understanding of how urban informalities operate in order to design appropriate (responsive) strategies and policies.

Using the lens of *urban metabolism*, the city is seen as an ecosystem with various resources flowing through it.[3] This surpasses the concept based on an analogy of an organism's metabolism with inputs and outputs, as the city cannot be reduced to a single organism. On the contrary, the overlaying of various system components, each with its inflows and outflows, adds to the complexity of urban reality. The overall aim of using the concept of urban metabolism is to create a naturalesque metabolism advocating a cyclical nature rather than a linear one, to focus on resource management.[4] Hence, this article investigates current resource flows through material flow analysis from source to sink in two diverse districts in Cairo, a formal district and an informal one, regarding materials (waste). The aim is to understand flows in these districts and propose locally responsive interventions that address local priorities to counter citywide one-size-fits-all solutions. Overlaying quantified resource flows and Quality of Life (QOL) assessment is important to highlight how resources are being utilized to provide livability.[5]

It is obvious that within low-income countries, resource consumption is low, but so is the livability standard, which reflects an advancement not in being greener but in being poorer. On the other hand, more affluent cities are very high consumers of resources, leading to resource depletion if more cities were to pursue the same consumption pattern.

From the various approaches to quantify urban metabolism, the cited work adopts the material flow analysis method, which covers the whole life cycle within an urban system, linking it to redesigning the city. The cited research project relies on parcel audits, which are embedded in an urban metabolism information system (UMIS) developed by the Ecocity Builders NGO and partners, through a joint project with Cairo University. Since the project was conducted in a data-scarce environment with a participatory action research approach, the methodology coupled crowd-sourced data, parcel audits, and expert knowledge to better understand resource flows based on a bottom-up approach, as opposed to relying on national governmental data. The research further correlated the perceived quality of life in the investigated areas

and the actual resource flows. It utilized fieldwork investigations to argue against the local misconceptions regarding the inefficiency of informal areas/systems versus the higher efficiency of planned areas/systems.

As more than twenty million people reside in the Greater Cairo region, the surge of resources reflects the exponential urban growth and related increase in consumption, a situation that requires both better management of supply as well as reconfiguring demand. The city has a wide urban spectrum, from formally planned districts to informal, unplanned ones. Research identified two districts in Cairo that represent opposite ends on the urban scale: Imababa and Zamalek. The district of Imbaba, with around one million inhabitants (mostly low to middle income) and a density of 600 inhabitants per hectare, is representative of the majority of Cairo's informal districts. The Zamalek district, an island, is part of the upscale city core with greater numbers of middle- to high-income households, 17,000 inhabitants, and only 121 inhabitants per hectare.

Through roundtable discussions with local community organizations and representatives, the inhabitants of each district selected different resources to investigate. The focus here is on material waste, which was a third priority in Imbaba but a first priority in Zamalek. For the material (waste) flow investigation, a number of household/parcel audits were conducted covering different archetypes in each area. Basically, each household was asked how much waste they discard on average per week for different materials (including paper, organics, plastics, textiles, glass, metal, wood, yard trimmings, appliances, hazardous waste, inerts, and other). Afterward, an investigation was conducted into what happens to the materials from their source until they reach the household—the upstream—and what happens to the materials after leaving the household until they reach the sink/infill or are recycled—the downstream.[6] By comparing results from both districts and across different land use, and focusing on the demand indicator of the Sankey diagrams,[7] it is apparent that the consumed materials differ dramatically within the same area for different uses (residential, commercial, educational, hotels, etc.) as well as between different areas regarding size and type (paper, organic, metal, glass, plastic, textile, etc.). This finding contradicts the current conviction that a single waste management system could be devised in different parts of the city and have the same efficiency. The current waste accumulation on most streets of Cairo is a witness to the failure of a one-size-fits-all system. Moreover, the variance in recycling rates of the two districts within the downstream processes reflects the reality of the waste components. Interestingly, in both districts the Quality

of Life QOL assessment reported the inadequate quality of the environment relating to the accumulation of waste piles on streets for days. Thus, revealing the municipality's inability to dispose adequately of the generated waste and the irresponsiveness of the system to the difference in waste composition, size, and recycling rate.

Remarkably, despite Imbaba's low rate of per capita waste generation and recycling, attributed to the community's lower affluence and their typical reuse of materials prior to discarding, the massive total amount of waste requiring significant management is a result of the enormous population size. Local waste management facilities distributed among small vacant parcels to collect, sort, and store until the pickup of municipal waste could be a more efficient and hygienic system. Such facilities could be combined with small parklets that would use recycled materials for furniture and recreational elements for children, thus fulfilling a need identified in the QOL assessment.

Interestingly, the informal system of waste collectors in Zamalek, with recycling rates of 70 to 80 percent, excluding organic waste, has surpassed the recycling rates of a formal system that has been trying to take over for the past fifteen years, in which most materials end up in landfills. Such an efficient system should be embraced rather than excluded from the waste management system, and in

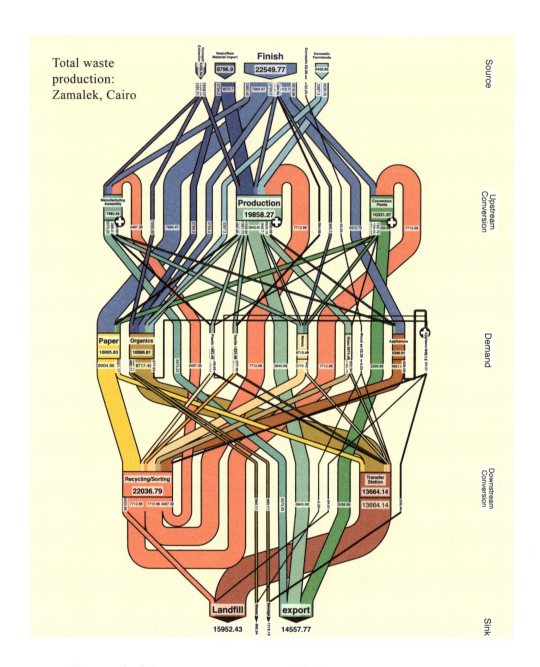

Total waste production: Zamalek, Cairo

Zamalek's more-recyclable waste attracts informal waste collectors.

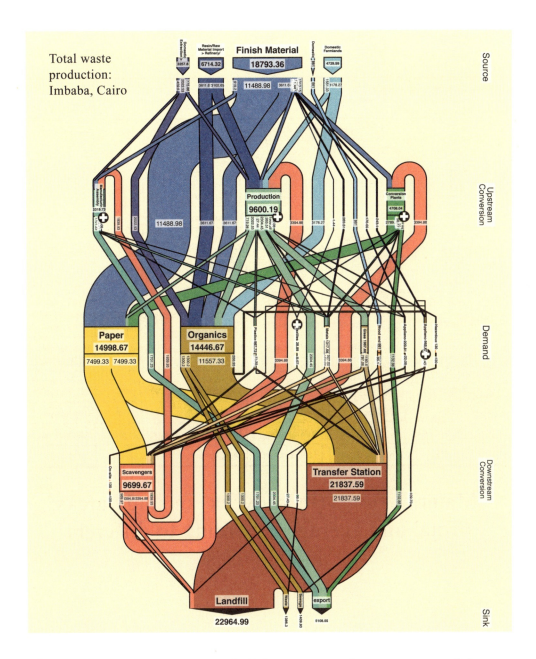

Total waste production: Imbaba, Cairo

Imbaba's less-recyclable waste is managed by the local municipality and mostly ends up in landfills.

| Area | Per capita/user consumption by material type | Total for study area | Average residential | Average commercial | Average educational | Average hotel |
|------|------|------|------|------|------|------|
| Imbaba | Paper | 1.65 kg/capita | 1.83 kg/capita | 0.63 kg/user | Not existing | Not existing |
| | Organic | 1.59 kg/capita | 1.67 kg/capita | 1.2 kg/user | | |
| | Metal | 0.14 kg/capita | 0.17 kg/capita | 0.02 kg/user | | |
| | Glass | 0.22 kg/capita | 0.13 kg/capita | 0.72 kg/user | | |
| | Plastic | 0.06 kg/capita | 0.04 kg/capita | 0.19 kg/user | | |
| | Textile | 0.003 kg/capita | 0 kg/capita | 0.02 kg/user | | |
| | Appliances | 0.086 kg/capita | 0.065 kg/capita | 0.21 kg/user | | |
| | Total | 3.749 kg/capita | 3.9 kg/capita | 2.99 kg/user | | |
| Zamalek | Paper | 1.62 kg/capita | 2.4 kg/capita | 12.84 kg/user | 0.02 kg/user | 0.36 kg/user |
| | Organic | 1.76 kg/capita | 5.03 kg/capita | 0.44 kg/user | 0.01 kg/user | 0.34 kg/user |
| | Metal | 0.76 kg/capita | 0.99 kg/capita | 6.61 kg/user | 0.04 kg/user | 0.05 kg/user |
| | Glass | 0.5 kg/capita | 1.4 kg/capita | 0.24 kg/user | 0.01 kg/user | 0 kg/user |
| | Plastic | 0.32 kg/capita | 0.53 kg/capita | 1.25 kg/user | 0.09 kg/user | 0.38 kg/user |
| | Textile | 0.31 kg/capita | 0.82 kg/capita | 0.45 kg/user | 0.004 kg/user | 0.06 kg/user |
| | Appliances | 1.00 kg/capita | 0.88 kg/capita | 12.69 kg/user | 0.003 kg/user | 0.24 kg/user |
| | Total | 6.27 kg/capita | 12.05 kg/capita | 34.52 kg/user | 0.177 kg/user | 1.43 kg/user |

# Material flows (in kg/week) in study areas: Total and average according to different audited uses.

addition, a careful handling of organic waste should be adopted in order to counter current on-street accumulation that ends up in landfills. Two solutions could benefit Cairo: first, composting organic waste to provide fertilizer for surrounding agricultural fields and the increasing numbers of urban and roof top farms; second, transforming waste to energy within relevant power plants for eventual district-level distribution, advocating decentralized energy production and improved resilience of the energy network while reducing costs and capitalizing on local resources.

The previous approaches and related interventions support demand-driven solutions (sometimes even utilizing informal systems) rather than the current supply side policies and programs. This is an essential approach that responds to the need for enhancing livability in Cairo and other cities of the Global South. It is essential to look into one's locality, learn from it, and devise locally tailored solutions if sustainable development is ever to be realized. In addition, it is important to always create downstream value for resources to ensure an efficient circular metabolic system.

1  K. Schwab, ed., *Insight Report: The Global Competitiveness Report 2017–2018* (Geneva: World Economic Forum, 2017).
2  M. Fischer-Kowalski, M. Swilling, E. U. von Weizsäcker, et al., *Decoupling Natural Resource Use and Environmental Impacts from Economic Growth: A Report of the Working Group on Decoupling to the International Resource Panel* (UNEP, 2011).
3  Y. Zhang, "Urban Metabolism: A Review of Research Methodologies," *Environmental Pollution* 178 (2013): 463–73.
4  P. H. Brunner, "Reshaping Urban Metabolism," *Journal of Industrial Ecology* 11 (February 2007): 11–13.
5  Sahar Attia and Heba Allah E. Khalil, "Urban Metabolism and Quality of Life in Informal Areas," in *Plan Together – Right Now – Overall: From Vision to Reality for Vibrant Cities and Regions; Proceedings of REAL CORP 2015, 20th International Conference on Urban Development, Regional Planning and Information Society,* ed. M. Schrenk, V. V. Popovich, P. Zeile, et al. (Vienna: REAL CORP, 2015), 661–74.
6  FAO, *Forest Products 2010–2014* (Rome: Food and Agricultural Organization of the United Nations, 2014); Hari Goyal, "Paper & Paperboard Production & Consumption for Egypt," 2015, Pulp & Paper Resources & Information Site, http://www.paperonweb.com/Egypt.htm; Nader Noureddin, "Egypt's Food Needs," *Al-Ahram Weekly*, November 24–30, 2016, http://weekly.ahram.org.eg/News/18897.aspx; "Egypt," Observatory of Economic Complexity, last accessed October 16, 2019, https://oec.world/en/profile/country/egy/.
7  A Sankey diagram shows the flow of a resource from one point to the other, where the width of the arrow represents the size of the resource at that stage.

# Toward Urban Dematerialization: Governance for the Urban Commons

Mark Swilling

Virtually every international meeting about the future of cities proceeds from a UN statistic which states that the global urban population is expected to almost double between 2010 and 2050. The New Urban Agenda adopted in Quito in 2016 accepts this as inevitable and suggests a set of relatively mild guidelines for how this can be achieved without destroying the planetary resources that urban economies depend on. This way of thinking builds on Sustainable Development Goal 11, adopted as part of the SDGs in 2015: "Make cities inclusive, safe, resilient and sustainable."

Cities, however, are built using large quantities of natural materials. The global study I coordinated on behalf of the International Resource Panel, *The Weight of Cities*, was the first attempt of its kind to quantify the materials currently in use in the world's urban systems, projected forward to 2050.[1] Over the next thirty years, 2.4 billion people will join the global urban population, meaning an increase from 54 percent of the population living in cities in 2015 to 68 percent by 2050. This will result in the significant expansion of existing cities as well as the construction of new ones. Consequently, material consumption is predicted to grow faster than urban populations.

Quantitative analysis of the global resource requirements of future urbanization shows that without a new approach, material consumption by the world's cities will grow from forty billion tons in 2010 to around ninety billion tons by 2050. In their construction and operation, and to support urban lifestyles, cities use billions of tons of raw materials, from fossil fuels, sand, gravel, and iron ore to biotic resources such as wood and food. The high demand for such raw materials far exceeds what the planet can provide. Resources should now become a central policy concern. Furthermore, the long-term historic de-densification trend of 2 percent per year (i.e., that cities are becoming less compact) threatens to increase global urban land use from just below one million km² to over 2.5 million km² by 2050, putting agricultural land and food supplies at risk.

The *Weight of Cities* report proposes three major interventions to halve urban resource requirements by 2050:

1. Introduction on a mass scale of resource-efficient urban infrastructure (specifically, bus rapid transit instead of passenger cars, green commercial buildings instead of conventional office blocks, and district energy instead of boilers and air conditioners). This could achieve a 24 to 47 percent reduction in impacts on water, energy, land, and metals by 2050 in comparison with a baseline for these sectors.

2. Reverse the century-long de-densification tendency using various interventions, resulting in a ten-fold reduction in resource consumption.

3. Implement new modes of urban governance that foster accelerated experimentation and innovation across all major urban sectors, with special attention to mobility, housing, food, and energy.

Urban dematerialization on this scale will not happen via market mechanisms alone. It will require purposeful interventions by public-sector institutions at different levels in order to ensure that the transitions are just and deep. However, this does not advocate for a return to a Weberian bureaucratic golden age where development is determined exclusively by the state. Instead, public-sector institutions should support the emergence of the urban commons—the shared physical and virtual spaces that conjoin within newly configured urban spaces and allow urban settlements to thrive in an environment of abundance and cultural flowering. Dematerialization, in this context, becomes the organizing framework for new modes of urban living, prosperity, and human flourishing.

In order to get a handle on how to address the quantified domestic material consumption of coming urbanization, it is important to recognize that the configuration of urban form and infrastructure, functions, and metabolisms has changed several times and quite radically over the past 150 years. Appreciating this track record makes it easier to understand what may be emerging following the 2007–8 financial crisis as cities come to terms with the challenges of social inclusion and ecological sustainability.

Statistical evidence overwhelmingly supports the claim that modern urban patterns resulted in a drastic increase in resource requirements. Undoubtedly it was the combustion engine, and the car-oriented techno-infrastructure related to it, that was a catalyst for the resource-intensive Great Acceleration that intensified after the Second World War. Sprawled out urban forms interconnected by cheap car-based intra-urban mobility were the result of cities with modern aspirations. It was this that drove the transition from a dependence on biomass to a dependence on nonrenewables from the 1950s onward.[2] In terms of governance, it was tied to a managerial and hierarchical model of city planning, epitomized by the master planner of New York, Robert Moses, and Georges-Eugène Haussmann from nineteenth-century Paris.

The decline of human-development imperatives in favor of productivity and growth during the neoliberal era from the 1980s onward would not have been possible without computerization.[3] As China became the world's manufacturer, its financial surpluses were transformed into the credit that drove the consumer boom and the massive escalation of urban property values across most economies during the decade preceding the financial crisis of 2007.[4] But this financialized and short-term-oriented form of global capitalism is now haunted by the negative side effects it has produced.

The economic transition from welfarist, Keynesian mass production to a neoliberal, post-Fordist, and debt-funded consumerism resulted in far-reaching changes in urban governance. These changes occurred during the 1980s and 1990s with respect to city-level state structures, modes of governance, and types of political leadership. Since 2009, a wave of changes is underway as a new ecology of actors emerge who share, in one way or another, the notion that urban futures depend on the reconfiguration of urban infrastructures, in both social and ecological terms. Sustainable Development Goal 11 best expresses this aspiration to rebalance urban economic productivity, human well-being, and sustainable resource use in cities. Once again, state structures, modes of governance, and political leadership can be expected to transform what can now be referred to as the information-based "SDG era."

1 Mark Swilling, Maarten Hajer, et al., *The Weight of Cities: Resource Requirements of Future Urbanization; Report for the International Resource Panel* (Paris, 2018).
2 Fridolin Krausmann et al., "Growth in Global Materials Use, GDP and Population during the 20th Century," *Ecological Economics* 68, no. 10 (2009): 2696–705.
3 Manuel Castells, *The Information Age: Economy, Society and Culture* (Oxford: Blackwell, 1997).
4 Joseph Stiglitz, *Freefall: Free Markets and the Sinking of the Global Economy* (London: Allen Lane, 2010).

# How Much Does Your Building (or Its Corresponding Infrastructure) Weigh?

Stefanie Weidner

What started as a provocative question, posed in the 1960s by R. Buckminster Fuller, probably became his most famous and most cited quote. In the years after World War II, building lightly was a necessity in order to master the challenges with which the building sector was confronted. However, it seems that since then architectural projects have rarely represented a responsible use of the earth's finite resources. Apart from prestigious objects like Burj Khalifa—a prime example of the extensive use of Australian sand—even conventional housing projects represent a large consumption of resources and needs to be reevaluated.

The building sector is responsible for 50 percent of global resource consumption, resulting in immense consequences for the natural environment.[1] With an average 2.2 metric tons of materials used per square meter for a standard single-family house in an industrialized country like Germany, providing housing annually for an additional 83 million people globally becomes an impossible endeavor.[2] If every person were granted an average of 40 m² living space, which is a typical size for industrial countries,[3] 7.4 billion tons of construction material would need to be extracted, transported, and built every year. This does not include infrastructure or work and educational spaces, which account for an even larger portion. And who is to say that those who join the global community shall be denied the industrial standard? As gross domestic product (GDP) numbers continue to increase, standards of living space rise, and with them the consumption of natural resources.

Certainly, saving operational energy during the lifetime use of a building, which has been a major trend in the building sector for some years now, is a very reasonable approach for creating sustainable development. But it takes forty years of operational energy to equalize the amount of energy that is built-in.[4] Taking into consideration that more energy than could ever be used would be available by solar power, it becomes obvious that instead of saving energy, decreasing the amount of our limited natural resources should really become our focus of study.

While working at the Institute for Lightweight Structures and Conceptual Design (ILEK) at the University of Stuttgart, my approach as an architect was strongly influenced by the future-oriented way of thinking of the pioneers who have directed the institute — Emil Mörsch, Jörg Schlaich, Frei Otto, and Werner Sobek — leading to my decision to dig deeper into the issue of resources in the built environment. In order to grasp the topic, the first step was to define the parameters of a sustainable urban structure and identify which of these are relevant for a resource-efficient urban structure and can be influenced by architects and engineers.

As visualized in the figure on page 203, I defined eighteen parameters for sustainable urban structures that were categorized in four major groups: residents, urban development, ecology, and location. Further, these can be subdivided in up to

100 subordinate variables, out of which I filtered those that are irrelevant in terms of resources and cannot be influenced by architects or engineers. In my analysis I identified the variables of land use, resource consumption of infrastructure and buildings, urban density, and urban formation as relevant for further investigation.

These variables will be put in relation on a virtual study site in order to answer the central research questions: What is the true figure for the resources and construction materials that are built into urban structures, and finally, depending on the density, which building structure is more resource-efficient?

The site measures 1,000 by 1,000 meters and its framing parameters are similar to those in Germany in terms of building substance, GDP, and climate conditions. Of all possible building typologies and urban formations, the study focuses on those that are representative of residential areas. This results in five different urban scenarios: two-story stand-alone single-family houses, twenty- and forty-story residential high-rise buildings, four-story apartment buildings in ribbon development, and six-story apartment buildings in block structures.

Since new urban environments are formed in various densities, these five building typologies will each be placed on the site in three different densities: 400 residents per km², representing a rural

Residents  Urban Development  Ecology  Location

Mobility  City- and Regional Planning  Consumption of Natural Resources  Connectivity

Housing  Policies  Emissions  Geology

Social Demands  Density  Urban Micro-Climate  Climate

Consumer Behaviour  Urban Environment  Economy

Demands on Urban Environment  Political Situation

Demographics

Parameters for a sustainable urban structure:
Black means the variable is relevant in terms of
resources, blue means the variable is
relevant for further investigation.

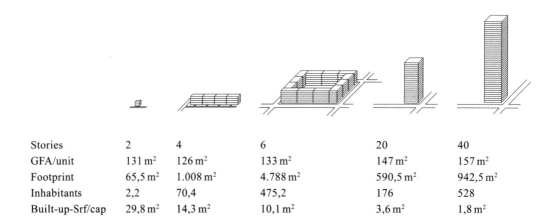

| | | | | | |
|---|---|---|---|---|---|
| Stories | 2 | 4 | 6 | 20 | 40 |
| GFA/unit | 131 m² | 126 m² | 133 m² | 147 m² | 157 m² |
| Footprint | 65,5 m² | 1.008 m² | 4.788 m² | 590,5 m² | 942,5 m² |
| Inhabitants | 2,2 | 70,4 | 475,2 | 176 | 528 |
| Built-up-Srf/cap | 29,8 m² | 14,3 m² | 10,1 m² | 3,6 m² | 1,8 m² |

# Five different case studies
# with respective data.

area; 4,000 residents per km², representing a typical density for medium-sized cities with one to four million inhabitants; and 20,000 residents per km², representing very dense urban structures such as Paris or Barcelona. In summary, this leads to fifteen different case studies.

Household units in this study measure 88 m² and accommodate a mean 2.2 residents, as is roughly the case for the 28 EU countries.[5] Based on these specifications, the first parameter, the consumption of natural resources, land area can be quantified. Data acquired so far, which forms the foundation of my future research, is summarized in the figure on page 204. It is notable that construction, circulation, and technical area vary with different building height, and the relation between net and gross floor area varies accordingly. Thus, building efficiency decreases with rising building height while the built-up area per person shrinks.

The main question regarding the resource consumption of residential buildings and their corresponding infrastructure still needs to be answered and discussed, since my research remains incomplete. However, the framing conditions are set and will enable a quantitative and qualitative analysis.

Quantifying the resource consumption of a building is a complex undertaking, which leads me back to my initial question: How much does your building weigh? During my research, I discovered a huge lack of knowledge about quantities in the built environment, especially when compared to an accurate documentation of economic aspects, for example. But this should not remain unknown. The scarcity of our natural resources can no longer be denied or ignored, especially as illegal and environmentally damaging sand mining continues in many parts of the world. Awareness and public transparency is more important than ever. I hope that by its completion, this research will help architects and engineers understand the impacts of their work and sensitize them for a more responsible handling of our natural resources.

1 M. Fischer-Kowalski, M. Swilling, E. U. von Weizsäcker, et al., *Decoupling Natural Resource Use and Environmental Impacts from Economic Growth: A Report of the Working Group on Decoupling to the International Resource Panel* (UNEP, 2011).
2 H. Lehmann and C. Stanetzky, "Zukunftsfähiges Bauen heißt Ressourcennutzung optimieren," in *Das Wuppertal Haus* (Basel: Birkhäuser, 1999);
3 United Nations, Department of Economic and Social Affairs, Population Division, *World Population Prospects: The 2017 Revision, Key Findings and Advance Tables* (United Nations, 2017), 53.
4 G. J. Treloar, P. E. D. Love, R. Fay, and B. Ilozor, "An Analysis of the Embodied Energy of Office Buildings by Height," *Facilities* 19 (2001): 204–14.
5 "Europäische Union: Durchschnittliche Haushaltsgröße in den Mitgliedsstaaten im Jahr 2018 (in Personen pro Haushalt)," Statista, https://de.statista.com/statistik/daten/studie/350573/umfrage/haushaltsgroesse-in-den-eu-laendern/.

# Cities as Ecosystems and Buildings as Living Organisms

Christoph Küffer

The building industry is a major driver of environmental destruction, responsible for 40 percent of global energy consumption and one of the main agents of anthropogenic climate change. The Intergovernmental Panel on Climate Change (IPCC) claims we must reach net-zero $CO_2$ emissions around 2050 to avoid dangerous climate change. Construction uses huge amounts of rapidly depleted materials such as gravel, sand, steel, wood, and water. Moreover the way in which we build cities encourages a resource-intensive lifestyle. Despite the urgent need for a radical reversal in material consumption rates, more than a doubling of annual demand for new materials is projected for the world's cities in the next few decades, thus eliminating potential gains in energy and material efficiency. As a consequence we

must rapidly transform urbanization and construction. Such a transformation might depend on four pillars: the end of growth, inclusive and equitable development, a circular economy, and the regeneration of social and natural capital to facilitate a transition toward a post-growth society. An inclusive and equitable development grants basic human needs and rights, such as food, water, health, peace, education, freedom and equality, dignity, social participation, and culture, to all citizens of the planet rather than fulfilling the false demands of an affluent minority. A circular economy must be built entirely on recycling, reuse, and upcycling, making such modes of production and consumption the norm, not the exception, and we must develop ways of material extraction, consumption, and reuse that regenerate rather than destroy natural and social capital. These aspirations are not new, and there will be no simple or single solution. Our established socioeconomic system of growth, consumption, inequality, and destructive extraction paralyzes action and creative and critical thinking, while taboos hinder open and critical engagement with the crisis of our society. Nevertheless, recent renewed interest in nature-based solutions and biophilic cities can help us envision alternative ways of building cities, and natural materials such as clay, wood, bamboo, or mycelium can inspire architects.

Urban nature's ecosystem services are acknowledged as central pillars of sustainable and healthy cities. Catchwords such as bio-design, responsive materials, adaptable architecture, and living systems reflect the growing respect for nature's design principles. But are these trends more than nature romanticized? Do they represent more than an unrealistic return to a dream of nature? Are they merely some kind of green washing? That is, do these systems imply sustainability by greening an otherwise unchanged destructive system? Biophilic design can indeed help transform the way we build cities if we critically challenge our design paradigms by learning from nature. Natural systems are characterized by codependent parts that dynamically shape each other; they are not a set of static and standardized parts designed independently of specific

contexts. Moreover, evolution — nature's engine of innovation — continuously improves existing solutions and cherishes slow-grown innovations rather than providing dreams of disruptive novelty. Nature's designs are also characterized by a high multifunctionality of imperfect solutions, which are the result of bricolage rather than the work of specialists that focus on controllability and optimized monofunctionality. Finally, urban citizens must relearn the eco-competence of living among other species with respect to the laws of ecology. This requires craftsmanship, tolerance, patience, responsibility, and humility.

Interdependencies

Embedded in their environment, living organisms follow the demands of the environment rather than expecting the environment to follow their demands. Wild species do shape the local environment, but only a few attempt to completely reconstruct the environment according to their needs. Rather, wild species and their environment depend on each other through dynamic feedback: organisms such as plants influence the environmental conditions under which they live — such as the local climate, elemental cycles, or the composition of the atmosphere (in our time most notably $CO_2$ concentration) — while being simultaneously affected by them and constantly forced to adapt through self-healing, plasticity of their phenotype, learning, and rapid evolution. Such a dialogic relationship between organisms and the environment can be circular (e.g. recycling) or lead to directional change (e.g. succession).

Construction and city design often neglect the potentials of locally rooted interdependencies. For instance, in nature soils maintain plant life and the decaying plant material in return feeds the soil. In green cities, the soil (i.e. the clay of an earth building) and the vegetation layers (i.e. the green facade or roof) are often separated from each other. As a consequence, natural materials (such as wood or clay) are extracted elsewhere in order to be used as dead building material, while ecological processes are maintained through artificial solutions and external inputs of resources (e.g. artificial fertilizers, pipes that supply water and nutrients, planting material that is collected from the wild or produced in garden centers). What would it mean instead to reconnect the two layers of the unearthed soil (earth buildings) and uprooted greenery (urban greenery) in buildings that function as three-dimensional ecosystems? How would such a reconstructed building (and ultimately city) ecosystem work? To what extent could the natural processes of soil formation, decomposition, nutrient cycling, plant colonization, rooting, animal life, water storage, evaporation, and succession be re-created? By

envisioning buildings as living organisms that are constantly evolving and responding to the environment while driven by the behavior of their organic parts (soil, vegetation, animals, humans).

Slow-Grown Innovation

In science and design we love novelty: technoscientific progress promises new and improved solutions. No doubt, breakthrough innovations open up new possibilities, but they often also result in unexpected negative impacts to the environment, our health, and/or social life. Nature's engine of innovation — evolution — continuously improves existing solutions and adapts them to different and changing environments. Indeed, a responsible innovation process does not end at the doors of the design office or the laboratory, it anticipates the impacts on the environment and society and continues as a trial-and-error learning process during implementation within different contexts. Conversely, novelty often leads to more costs than benefits. Our society externalizes these costs by imposing them on nature, the poor, future generations, or distant places. On an interconnected and densely packed planet, externalizing social and ecological costs becomes impossible, and was always ethically questionable. In the Anthropocene, therefore, we must gain a renewed appreciation for tradition and heritage that results from long-term learning and slow innovation in outdoor real-world laboratories. Often it is better to safeguard and transform the existing rather than replace it with novel untested solutions. We know enough—we must face the challenges of how to upscale and responsibly implement long-known solutions.

Bricolage

Evolution does not produce perfect solutions, it rather produces good-enough solutions that serve multiple purposes simultaneously and emerge from an innovation environment of multiple constraints (limited resources, time restrictions, unpredictable environments, existing designs, and coexistent solutions of other species). Nature's provisional, experimental, and pragmatic solutions are the result of bricolage, which allows for self-organized, context-sensitive, integrative, and dynamic design processes that value diversity. Indeed, in nature, diversity—of genes, organisms, ecological functions, species interactions, abiotic structures, and materials—enables resilience. Specialists that focus on controllability and optimized monofunctionality—thereby reducing diversity—might be less apt for a time of radical and rapid change and manifold crises than tinkerers of all kinds such as those living in informal settlements or other marginalized places. Reversing the

technology transfer process by learning from the poor and marginalized, including refugees and indigenous peoples, might help us redesign our modern cities.

Eco-competence

We must all relearn to live among other species and in line with the laws of ecology. No architect will design a building without structural analysis. Equally, bio-design and its uses must abide by the laws of ecology. This means foremost that ecology must become an integral part of curricula in architecture, design, and engineering. Eco-competence also means that we relearn to live in environments that are alive, which requires rejecting a culture of unlimited demands and externalized liability to embrace a culture of craftsmanship, tolerance, patience, responsibility, and humility. The maintenance of a lawn can be outsourced to the artificial fertilizer, lawnmower, standardized seed mixture, and pesticides. Such a lawn is intended to reflect perfectly the expectations of the owner—uniform green, no weeds, low costs, no bugs—and for any potential problem an external expert exists to offer a quick fix. But such lawns are ecologically dead. Species-rich flower tapestries—a colorful form of lawn—in contrast maintain healthy soils and provide flowers to pollinators while serving as playgrounds and displays of wealth. However, they require eco-competence and patience on the part of the owner in caring for his or her land.

might become tomorrow's recreational areas for city inhabitants. Cities will become ecosystems, with buildings as their living organisms.

## Conclusions

Nature can help us envision cities for a post-growth society embedded in a circular economy that recycles, reuses, and upcycles all materials and is fueled by solar energy. Such cities will be alive in the sense that their parts mutually and dynamically shape each other. They will value tradition, heritage, and the existing, and they will be designed through bricolage to produce local multifunctional solutions. Architects must construct provisional, adaptive, and porous buildings that allow daylight, fresh air, fluctuating temperatures, and wildlife to move more freely between internal and external spaces. City inhabitants must accept that untamed natural processes co-shape their cities and the interior environments of their buildings. And construction could change from an industry that extracts, transports, uses, and disposes of materials to a service industry that cares for living materials — akin to gardening — by focusing on their reuse, upcycling, disassembly, and reassembly. A decentralized organization is needed to develop context-sensitive, adaptable solutions in partnerships with local users and stakeholders. Where extraction and disposal of materials remains necessary, ecological regeneration of the affected land should be an integral part of the industry, so that quarries and waste-disposal sites

# From Manual to Digital and Vice Versa: Digitization, Labor, and Construction

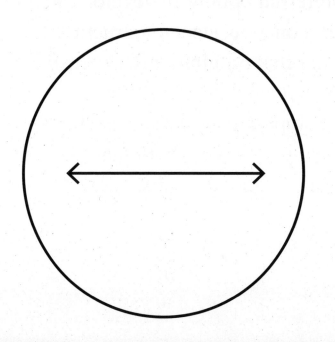

Reducing the waste and emissions of the construction industry will require the fields of architecture, engineering, and construction to work together.
By confronting a series of tensions—manual vs. digital, craft vs. machine, tradition vs. innovation—we can devise technical solutions and challenge what is typically considered appropriate.

Solutions must be adaptable to diverse economic, geographic, and political contexts: In advanced economies, with high labor costs, prefabrication may be the preferred option. In developing countries, concrete, steel, or structural timber are often prohibitively expensive or simply not available, but labor remains comparatively cheap, so smart use of local resources—both material and human—can yield substantial benefits.

A key factor in this debate will be digital design, which can help us devise more efficient construction methods, structural performance, and material quality.
But we must also consider the social importance of labor in our increasingly digitized world. Can we find a mix of digital and manual fabrication that embraces the advantages of both?

Anna Heringer
Philippe Block

# Imposing Challenges, Disruptive Changes: Rethinking the Floor Slab

Philippe Block, Cristián Calvo Barentin,
Francesco Ranaudo, Noelle Paulson

The United Nations Department of Economic and Social Affairs estimates that by 2050 the world's population will have increased by over 2.1 billion people.[1] Providing housing and infrastructure for them would require building an amount equivalent to what currently exists. It is simply not possible to continue building the way we do today. Though the field and broader public have been slow to take notice of the building industry's contribution to the environmental crisis, it is now finally receiving increased attention. Bill and Melinda Gates emphasized the problem succinctly in their foundation's 2019 annual letter: "The world's building stock is expected to double by 2060—the equivalent of adding another New York City monthly between now and then. That's a lot of cement and steel. We need to find a way to make it all without worsening climate change."[2]

To appropriately confront this urgent environmental crisis, the building industry faces three grand challenges: (1) reducing pollution, specifically carbon dioxide emissions; (2) slowing the depletion of natural resources; and (3) minimizing waste production.

The challenge of pollution refers first and foremost to embodied emissions, since efforts to reduce this lag behind what has already been achieved to reduce operational emissions.[3] According to the research of Catherine De Wolf, there are two main design approaches that may be applied to achieve the reduction of embodied carbon in a building: (i) build with less

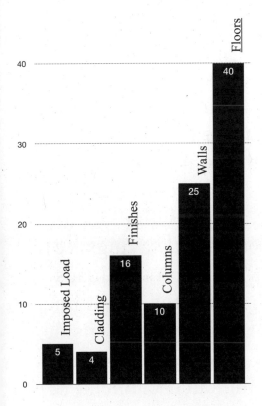

Typical weight distribution considered in the design of a residential reinforced concrete high-rise frame construction.

volume of materials in all layers and (ii) use materials with a low embodied carbon coefficient.[4] The global-warming potential of a building (GWP, expressed in $kgCO_2e/m^2$) can then be calculated by multiplying both variables. Even in a medium-height multistory building the structural mass accounts for as much as three-quarters of the total design loads (see graph to the left); our research focuses on this area.[5]

The second challenge of resource depletion focuses on the resources needed to produce the planet's most commonly used building material: (steel-)reinforced concrete.[6] Mining beaches, riverbeds, or the sea floor for the type of rough, large-grained sand needed as the aggregate in concrete has detrimental effects on shorelines and ecosystems, not to mention the fact that such sand is a finite natural resource.[7]

The third challenge centers on the material waste produced during and after construction and what may result as a part of the design. In the European Union, 25 to 30 percent of all waste produced by humans — approximately 800 million tons per year — comes from construction and demolition.[8] Some estimates indicate that up to 30 percent of the total weight of materials brought to construction sites finishes as waste, even for simple geometries;[9] the amount of waste can increase exponentially during the construction of more

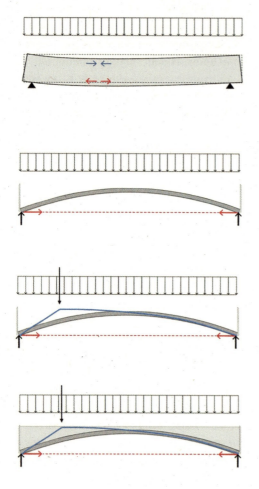

Funicular floor concept: (a) standard concrete element resisting applied loads through bending action; (b) the same load is resisted through funicular (i.e., compression-only) action with dramatic material savings; (c) concentrated loads modify the thrust line, which is now outside the section of the funicular element; (d) material is reintroduced (in the stiffening rib) to enclose the thrust line.

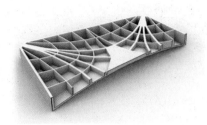

Current layout proposal for HiLo project to be built on the NEST platform on the Empa campus in Dübendorf, Switzerland.

geometrically complex structures, which may require bespoke formworks that are disposed of after their single use.

Based on the concept of "strength through geometry," and particularly because of its vaulted, compression-only form, the funicular floor developed by the Block Research Group at ETH Zurich is able to confront these challenges.[10] It shows that, enhanced by computation and complemented with digital fabrication, much-needed improvements to the status quo can be attained through structural design. This is achieved by employing the following effective measures:

– Its optimized stiffened shell geometry significantly reduces the structural

volume required by placing material only where needed—that is, following the flow of forces under all loading cases. All common structural slab solutions (flat slabs, ribbed slabs, hollow core slabs, predalles, etc.) use bending action to resist applied loads, resulting in an inefficient use of material due to cross-section partialization. For this reason, standard floor slabs usually make up half of a multistory building's structural mass. Compared to a typical solid floor of reinforced concrete, the funicular floor saves up to 70 percent of material. That is analogous to removing more than one-third of the entire structural mass of a multistory building, resulting in a chain reaction of improvements to other structural elements, easier transport of materials and components to the site, and simpler construction logistics.

– Its funicular form enables the use of low-strength materials, ten or more times fewer than those required by structural systems working in bending, even for reduced structural sections. Given that there is a direct relation between the strength of a material and its embodied carbon,[11] reducing stresses immediately impacts De Wolf's equation by lowering the embodied energy of the materials used. Furthermore, the low material-strength requirements facilitate the use of low- or negative-embodied carbon alternatives. These may offer the most effective strategy, since, as the

# Unreinforced rib-stiffened concrete funicular floor prototype.

different carbon scenarios in the 2018 Intergovernmental Panel on Climate Change report shows, reducing to zero emissions by 2050 is imperative.[12]

– Decoupling compression and tension flows not only reduces internal strain incompatibilities but also allows materials to remain separated. This can result in increased longevity, since easier access to components better facilitates their replacement while also providing less wasteful corrosion and fire protection strategies. Furthermore,

single-material systems allow for easier recycling and can prevent downcycling.[13]

– Discretization strategically keeps the force flow in compression under all loading cases by releasing bending stresses in specific locations. In addition to controlling force flow, large settlements of the supports will not result in internal stresses. When detailing is done carefully—for example, without using adhesives—a straightforward disassembly can be imagined, potentially contributing to a more circular economy.

– Prefabrication allows for the efficient use of digital fabrication, such as bespoke, 3-D-printed formworks constructed from fully recyclable materials. When applied to the floor slab and facilitated by advances in computational structural design and digital fabrication, the presented strategies confront these challenges and offer opportunities for necessary, disruptive innovation. When we ask how we can balance the need to build shelter for an ever-increasing human population with the hard facts of the pollution and waste caused by our industry, we are compelled to rethink how we design and build. Furthermore, we must reckon with how we teach architecture and engineering, and even how we might modify building codes to allow for greater flexibility. There is reason for cautious optimism, but the urgency of the situation requires diligence, awareness, and openness to change from all parts of the industry.[14]

1 "World Population Projected to Reach 9.8 Billion in 2050, and 11.2 Billion in 2100," United Nations Department of Economic and Social Affairs, June 21, 2017, https://www.un.org /development/desa/en/news/population/world -population-prospects-2017.html.
2 Bill Gates and Melinda Gates, "Our 2019 Annual Letter," *Gates Notes*, February 12, 2019, https:// www.gatesnotes.com/2019-Annual-Letter.
3 Catherine De Wolf, Michael Ramage, and John Ochsendorf, "Low Carbon Vaulted Masonry Structure," *Journal of the International Association for Shell and Spatial Structures*, no. 57 (2016): 275; Catherine De Wolf, "Low Carbon Pathways for Structural Design: Embodied Life Cycle Impacts of Building Structures" (PhD diss., Massachusetts Institute of Technology, 2017); Taofeeq Ibn-Mohammed et al., "Operational vs. Embodied Emissions in Buildings: A Review of Current Trends," *Energy and Buildings*, no. 66 (2013): 232–45.
4 De Wolf, "Low Carbon Pathways for Structural Design."
5 Chi Kwan Chau et al., "Assessment of $CO_2$ Emissions Reduction in High-Rise Concrete Office Buildings Using Different Material Use Options," *Resources, Conservation and Recycling*, no. 61 (2012): 22–34.
6 Michael F. Ashby, *Materials and the Environment: Eco-informed Material Choice*, 2nd ed. (Oxford: Butterworth-Heinemann, 2013).
7 "Sand and Sustainability: Finding New Solutions for Environmental Governance of Global Sand Resources," Global Resource Information Database – Geneva, May 2019, https://unepgrid.ch/sand/.
8 "Construction and Demolition Waste," *European Commission*, http://ec.europa.eu/environment /waste/construction_demolition.htm (last updated August 7, 2019); and "Resource Efficient Use of Mixed Wastes," *European Commission*, http:// ec.europa.eu/environment/waste/studies/mixed _waste.htm (last updated August 7, 2019).
9 Mohamed Osmani, "Construction Waste," in *Waste: A Handbook for Management*, ed. Trevor Letcher and Daniel Vallero (Cambridge, MA: Academic Press, 2011), 207–18.
10 Philippe Block et al., *Beyond Bending: Reimagining Compression Shells* (Munich: Edition DETAIL, 2017).
11 Ashby, *Materials and the Environment*; Guillaume Habert and Nicolas Roussel, "Study of Two Concrete Mix-Design Strategies to Reach Carbon Mitigation Objectives," *Cement and Concrete Composites*, no. 31 (2009): 397–402.
12 "Special Report on Global Warming of 1.5°C, 2018," Intergovernmental Panel on Climate Change (IPCC), https://www.ipcc.ch/sr15/ (accessed May 21, 2019).
13 Michael Braungart and William McDonough, *Cradle to Cradle: Remaking the Way we Make Things* (New York: North Point Press, 2002).
14 Amanda Schaffer, "The Climate Optimist: Susan Solomon," *MIT Technology Review*, February 21, 2019, https://www.technologyreview .com/s/612803/the-climate-optimist/.

# Pizza and Dirt in Uganda: A Student-Led Project Proves the Viability of Rammed-Earth Construction

Achilles Ahimbisibwe

Most Ugandans live in impoverished villages or urban slums, in run-down homes crafted from mud, wood, tin, and low-quality bricks. But our architecture schools do little to promote building for such contexts, instead preferring to train graduates to design for the affluent elites in a handful of cities—missing vast opportunities to create more sustainable communities.

At the Faculty of the Built Environment at Uganda Martyrs University, we focus on holistic education and a neighborhood-scale approach aimed at helping communities better understand and manage their natural and built environments. Energy use, waste management, material production, indoor comfort, and the aesthetic quality of materials all present opportunities for architects to contribute at a human scale. With guidance from Martin Rauch and Anna Heringer—pioneers in the field of earth and bamboo construction—the faculty developed what we call the Pizza Kiosk Project. The idea was to build a structure on our campus where we could deploy alternative materials that could be locally sourced and to understand their effect on the cost of building. The ultimate goal was to find ways to improve fuel efficiency at local kilns, increase the reuse of construction waste or salvaged materials, and raise awareness about the energy needed to create such buildings and the ongoing costs and energy needed for them.

The project gave our students experience working on a real site with an actual client. They designed a small pizza

Students building the pizza oven.

Cement-free plaster is added to protect the unfired bricks from surface moisture.

A technician demonstrates brick-laying techniques.

In the foreground, a counter made from rammed earth.

Mortar, plaster, and rammed-earth material are mixed in a tarpaulin.

The roof is supported by eucalyptus poles.

Clay is used as a binding agent because clay mixes are easier to wash off.

Cleaning up the site after construction.

The Pizza Kiosk Project shows that it's possible to transfer technology and skills to local artisans while increasing awareness of the environmental costs of building. The project has proven that when communities embrace alternative solutions such as rammed earth, innovative methods that are more suited to local needs can thrive.

and barbecue stand at the edge of our campus that used rammed-earth walls, stabilized soil blocks, and unfired clay bricks made on-site. All mortars used in the project were clay and sand variants meant to replace the cement mortar typical in our area. The idea was to form a business—selling pizza—that would give the project a higher profile in the university community and dispel lingering concerns about earth construction, which is often deemed less safe and durable than modern building methods. Undergraduate students were asked to critique the design and participate in the construction, which proved that such buildings can be constructed by mostly unskilled workers. This approach helped illustrate that it's possible to transfer technology and skills to local artisans while increasing awareness of the environmental costs of building.

We managed to salvage materials such as stone aggregates, gravel, clay, and sand at no cost from abandoned construction sites nearby, and all mixing was done with simple hand tools. We didn't have enough time to make and dry unfired clay bricks (which takes several months) before the end of the semester, so we bought some from a nearby manufacturer. And we had to purchase eucalyptus poles, roofing sheets, and cement (used to stabilize the earth blocks). Our aim was to recover those costs from running the pizza business, a strategy that helped us investigate the possibilities of crowd-sourced funding to pay for a project through a community enterprise. Expert trainers volunteered their time, and local residents provided artisanal labor in exchange for the opportunity to learn new earth techniques.

One unforeseen result was that patrons of the pizza kiosk spread the word about our rammed-earth wall, which has led to our participation in four other projects. For one in Kampala, local regulations didn't address earth walls so we had to prove that our construction methods were safe. After correspondence that lasted over a year, we got permission, and the wall was built in a day. We were then invited to take part in a pilot project for a two-story rammed-earth building in the Kampala suburb of Gayaza, which allowed us to train a further group of skilled artisans. These people could then teach new builders—which helped them get more involved in the construction and gain greater skills by tutoring the next team.

The adoption of alternative technologies faces frequent barriers: the bureaucracy of academia, regulatory statutes, the construction aspirations of local communities, and the opposition of entrenched producers of construction materials. But our project has proven that when communities embrace alternative solutions such as rammed earth, innovative methods that are more suited to local needs can thrive.

# Building Climate: From Mechanical to Material

Arno Schlueter

The growing awareness of buildings as significant consumers of resources, emitters of greenhouse gases, and contributors to phenomena such as urban heat islands has moved them to the center of global endeavors to mitigate climate change, transition toward renewable energy, and improve the well-being of populations in cities. Energy for a building is consumed in two principal ways: first, through the materials, from the harvesting of raw materials to the actual construction process, and second, through the operation of the building. Depending on the construction, climatic context, and building systems, the consumption of the latter could be a multiple of the former.

The energy used to operate a building serves a simple purpose: to keep the interior environment in a state that is healthy and comfortable for its occupants. In most locations around the world, the effects of outside conditions and our own contributions to the indoor environment, such as carbon dioxide, humidity, and heat, require flows of energy and mass in the building to maintain such a state. Heat needs to be moved, fresh air supplied, and contaminated air removed. Humidity, though not as critical as heat, cold, and light, should stay within certain thresholds.

The increasing demand for comfort has led to electromechanical systems for heating, cooling, air-conditioning, and lighting. Air-conditioning—the ability to design the indoor environment independent of the outdoors—is a transformative technology since it allows humans to pursue any occupation, anywhere, with similar productivity and effectiveness. The downside of air-conditioning is its high energy consumption and its function as a symbol of wealth and status, which drives its uptick, especially in emerging economies.

Before fossil fuels were made readily available, architects and builders had to rely on passive means to sustain comfort, even in harsh outdoor conditions, or choose among the few available renewable energy sources for heating, such as wood. Constructive responses to this challenge included massive walls made from earthen materials that incorporated small openings, bodies of water that provided evaporative cooling in hot and dry climates, light walls with large openings for passive ventilation in hot and humid regions, and double windows to create an air buffer in cold regions. Knowledge of materials and construction and their impact on a building's microclimate and the occupants' well-being were passed on as heuristics of the profession.

Cheap and accessible fossil fuels have rendered this knowledge almost irrelevant since they allow for conditioning any space using electromechanical systems. These technical systems have advanced over the last decades, but their key principle of moving energy and mass using fans, pumps, air ducts, pipes, and vents remains the same. State-of-the-art building systems are able to provide a fine-grained response to interior demands and available energy sources on-site. Such systems, however, often come with increased costs and added complexity, which makes them challenging to plan, build, and operate.

Rethinking materials and their performative capacities opens up an alternative route. A deeper understanding of how their physical properties can be leveraged for environmental control and energy conversion could reduce systems complexity and offer entirely new options, both environmentally and architecturally. The application of photovoltaics — essentially a material technology — to the building envelope serves as an example. The large-scale application of building-integrated photovoltaics (BIPV) has become a key strategy to transform buildings toward carbon neutrality. New surface treatments of the BIPV's protective glass layer, such as color filters, open up new options for architectural design and construction, allowing photovoltaics to be treated as "solar material" and used for almost any material on the building envelope.

This development can be seen as a primer for the role of performative materials — however, it is still rooted in the traditional way of designing and constructing in a layered, linear process. Digital design and fabrication represent a fundamental shift in both design and process since they allow joint control of form, material choice, aggregation, geometry, and the surface of building elements. Functional capacities such as heat transfer and storage, air permeability, and humidity absorption and evaporation can be designed and fabricated as intrinsic properties of building elements such as envelopes, walls, floors, and ceilings, providing a bespoke response to the building's climatic and architectural context.

Functionally integrated building elements help reduce the complexity of mechanical systems, potentially reducing the energy needed to condition space to the occupants' needs and preferences. The impact is two-fold: these elements would not only conceive new, simple, robust yet efficient supply systems, but also, and more radically, conceptualize new building elements with custom functions such as walls that act as heat exchangers, facades that generate energy or regulate airflow, and columns that conduct electricity. The result will be new forms of hybrid building elements that are multifunctional, resource-efficient, and customizable. They can bridge passive and active approaches for indoor environmental control and energy supply.

Digital fabrication techniques will therefore allow for the conceptualization and creation of next-generation building systems for energy conversion and indoor environmental control by embedding performative capacities into building elements. In addition to reducing complexity, emissions, and costs, these techniques will reconnect aspects of energy and climate to architectural design and construction.

# Designing for Natural Ventilation: Climate – Architecture – System

Alpha Yacob Arsano

With the advancement of technology in the building industry, temperature regulation that was scarcely imaginable a few decades ago not only has become a reality in cities around the world, it has also led to an increase in energy and material consumption. Buildings in cities with hot climates now share similar technologies with ones located in cold or temperate climates. Climate-responsive building design that relies primarily on passive strategies to regulate interior temperature is being replaced by a new trend of active systems that require large amounts of energy and material.

Vernacular buildings are historical examples of passive systems: they respond to the climatic context using the available natural resources to create healthy and comfortable spaces for occupants. Before the expansive use of active building systems for heating, cooling, and ventilation, buildings were constructed in ways that would regulate the interior climate or temperature based on their overall form, the size of openings (windows, doors), and type of building envelope. However, in past decades the global trend has shifted. By the late 1960s, most new homes in the United States had central air conditioning, and window air-conditioners were more affordable than ever. Currently in middle-income countries, such as China, passive building systems are becoming obsolete, and a "new vernacular" is quickly spreading that heavily relies on active building systems. In 2013, more than eight times as many air-conditioning units were sold in China than in the United States.[1]

Energy use for cooling buildings has doubled between 2000 and 2018, led by a combination of warmer temperatures and population and economic growth, according to the International Energy Agency (IEA).[2] Owing to the rise of incomes and the wider use of appliances that generate heat, such as refrigerators and computers, buildings are increasingly adopting air-conditioning systems. Despite a wide range of climatic contexts, from extremely cold to extremely hot, air-conditioning units are installed in almost 90 percent of homes in the United States.[3] And this increase is also permeating regions where the use of active systems has not been common—for example, in India, whose population is four times that of the United States and where the need for cooling is twelve times as great. The IEA's 2018 report states that the number of AC units worldwide is predicted to increase from 1.6 billion to 5.6 billion by the middle of the century. As a result, the greenhouse-gas emissions from coal and natural-gas plants generating electricity to power the units will nearly double, from 1.25 billion tons in 2016 to 2.28 billion tons in 2050. Additionally, hydrofluorocarbons—the primary chemical compounds in AC units, which are leaked during their manufacturing, installation, and disposal[4]—are far more potent greenhouse gases than carbon dioxide, trapping thousands of times more heat in the atmosphere. Various publications on natural ventilation

have illustrated the important role of passive systems in reducing energy consumption in buildings. According to a study at Harvard University's Center for Green Buildings and Cities, up to 78 percent of cooling-energy consumption in China can be potentially reduced by natural ventilation, depending on the local weather and air quality.[5] However, without a process to design buildings that promotes a system combining active and passive strategies to reduce energy use and carbon emissions, new and retrofitted buildings will continue to shift to air-conditioning to maintain indoor thermal comfort.

Greenhouse-gas emissions from buildings can be reduced by taking a climate-responsive design approach: buildings in hot and dry climates should have different features than those in hot and humid or cold climates. Not all climates allow for passive strategies year round; however, in every climate natural ventilation in buildings can be used for a few weeks or months a year. To reduce emissions, a new way of thinking about building design is needed—a strategic, hybrid mode that permits both active and passive modes of operation.

Implementing strategies such as natural ventilation or thermal mass to regulate heat requires an analytic approach during the early stages of building design. Christoph Reinhart and I have created a support system

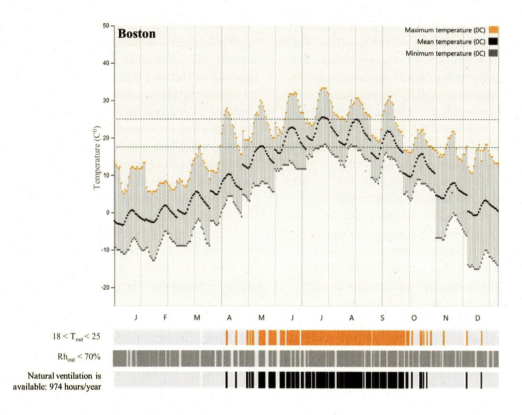

Evaluation of outdoor conditions in Boston
to predict the availability of natural ventilation.
The chart shows hourly maximum, minimum,
and mean temperatures from each month
of the year. The three bars indicate the hours
when the ambient temperature is between
18 and 25°C and when outdoor humidity is
less than 70 percent.

that is publicly accessible online. The user inputs the location or climate of the building project and its intended function (i.e., residence or office). The outdoor conditions are evaluated using the climate data of a project's location, and indoor conditions are assessed via an analytic calculation that predicts hourly indoor temperature.[6]

First, the analysis evaluates outdoor conditions such as ambient temperature and humidity to predict the availability of natural ventilation. Users can specify comfort requirements by adjusting the acceptable indoor temperature and humidity levels. Second, the analysis accounts for building parameters — envelope construction, thermal mass, and internal heat sources such as people, lighting, and equipment — which greatly influence indoor conditions. Actionable design goals are calculated and identified that will maintain occupants' thermal comfort preferences, with the intention to maximize the effectiveness of natural ventilation.

This web tool identifies feasible passive building strategies using natural ventilation. Direct ventilation is applicable when the daytime outdoor temperature is below the comfort threshold of the indoor temperature. When the outdoor temperature is too high, precooling and night ventilation are recommended. Precooling occurs

when natural ventilation is used to cool the indoor space a few hours before occupants are in the building when the outdoor temperature is relatively low — for instance, between 6:00 and 8:00 a.m. for a typical office — and night ventilation cools with natural ventilation at night — for instance, between 10:00 p.m. and 4:00 a.m. Once the recommended air-change rate is identified, ventilation can be easily and simply achieved owing to natural forces: airflow caused by wind or buoyancy. In the case that outdoor wind and buoyancy-driven ventilation aren't sufficient, fan-assisted airflow can be considered.

In order to produce buildings sustainably, with the lowest environmental impact possible, the early stages of the design process need to be considered.[7] Methodology to identify design goals that maximize the effectiveness of natural ventilation in hybrid buildings should be used to explore viable options that reduce energy use and carbon emissions. A publicly accessible, easy-to-use web tool facilitates the collaboration between stakeholders and clients. The primary input — climate data — is available online for over 10,000 locations around the world as of July 2019, enabling a wider application of the decision-support system.[8] The effort to maximize the use of passive strategies rather than solely relying on AC units is compatible with a goal set by the UN's Paris Agreement: to more than double the average energy efficiency of AC units worldwide between 2018 and 2050.[9]

1   Lucas W. Davis and Paul J. Gertler, "Contribution of Air Conditioning Adoption to Future Energy Use under Global Warming," *Proceedings of the National Academy of Sciences of the United States of America* 112, no. 19 (May 12, 2015): 5962–67, https://doi.org/10.1073/pnas.1423558112.
2   IEA, *The Future of Cooling: Opportunities for Energy-Efficient Air Conditioning* (Paris: IEA, 2018), https://doi.org/10.1787/9789264301993-en.
3   "2015 RECS Survey Data," Residential Energy Consumption Survey (RECS), U.S. Energy Information Administration, https://www.eia.gov/consumption/residential/.
4   Christina Ospina, "Cooling Your Home but Warming the Planet: How We Can Stop Air Conditioning from Worsening Climate Change," Climate Institute, August 7, 2018, https://climate.org/cooling-your-home-but-warming-the-planet-how-we-can-stop-air-conditioning-from-worsening-climate-change/.
5   Zheming Tong, Yujiao Chen, Ali Malkawi, Zhu Liu, and Richard B. Freeman, "Energy Saving Potential of Natural Ventilation in China: The Impact of Ambient Air Pollution," *Applied Energy*, no. 179 (October 2016): 660–68, https://doi.org/10.1016/j.apenergy.2016.07.019.
6   Alpha Yacob Arsano and Christoph Reinhart, *Early-Design Optimization of Target Ventilation Rates for Hybrid Buildings Using Single-Node Analytical Model* (Rome: IBPSA, 2019).
7   Luís Bragança, Susana M. Vieira, and Joana B. Andrade, "Early Stage Design Decisions: The Way to Achieve Sustainable Buildings at Lower Costs," *Scientific World Journal*, no. 2014 (2014), https://doi.org/10.1155/2014/365364.
8   See Dru Crawley and Linda Lawrie's website Climate.OneBuilding.Org, http://climate.onebuilding.org/.
9   IEA, *The Future of Cooling: Opportunities for Energy-Efficient Air Conditioning* (Paris: IEA, 2018), https://doi.org/10.1787/9789264301993-en.

# Rebuilding after Disaster: Children's Recreational Center in Juchitán, Oaxaca

Loreta Castro Reguera

Mexico's funnel-like form links the United States and Central America. At the northern border the width of the country is approximately 1,900 kilometers, and moving southward thins to 200 kilometers. This area, the Isthmus of Tehuantepec, is a low land that is vulnerable to strong winds, floods, and land movements.

In September 2017, a series of strong earthquakes hit Mexico. The seventh measured 8.2 on the Richter scale and its epicenter was in the Tehuantepec Gulf, near the Oaxacan coast. It dramatically affected the isthmian region, particularly the town of Juchitán de Zaragoza. According to the Ministry of Territory and Urban Development, 13,485 buildings in Juchitán were damaged and 2,240,400 tons of debris were produced, a disastrous

Most earthquakes in Mexico in 2018 occurred in the Tehuantepec region between Oaxaca, Chiapas, and Guerrero.

233

situation further exacerbated by flooding during the rainy season.

Different strategies were applied in an effort to rebuild the isthmian towns as quickly as possible, some of which ended up being more damaging than helpful. Short-sighted approaches neglected to plan for a long-term rebuilding process, dumped debris into local rivers, and reconstructed houses with cheap materials, disregarding traditional building methods that provide natural light, ventilation, and open spaces.

Juchitán has a population of 74,825 and is located in the state of Oaxaca in the southeast of the country. It is one of four towns located along the Los Perros River. The flatness of the land, a high rainfall (900 millimeters a year), and an underdeveloped drainage system lead to flooding in the urban areas during storms. Additionally, the isthmus is extremely vulnerable to earthquakes; in 2018, there were 30,350 tremors in Mexico, and 65.7 percent of them occurred in the state of Oaxaca.

Reconstruction after the September 2017 earthquakes meant not only rebuilding lost homes and public buildings but also addressing issues of flood prevention, debris disposal, construction efficiency, and the reuse of materials. The demolition of buildings had polluted the Los Perros River and the sewer infrastructure was highly damaged, provoking drastic health problems, especially during floods. The scarce number of public spaces in town, which are necessary for community cohesion during times of crisis, lacked basic maintenance.

Taller Capital was approached by the Mexico City office of MK Illumination, an Austrian lighting company, to refurbish a particular damaged public space in Juchitán with the aim of benefiting children. The local architecture firm Root Studio had been working on the reconstruction process in Juchitán. They led us to the Children's Recreational Center Hidalgo (CRI Hidalgo), which was partly reconstructed after having been severely damaged in the earthquake but still lacked a plan and money to refurbish the entire public space.

Together with Nadyeli Quiroz, who had been researching the effects of debris in the river and the region, Taller Capital formulated a hypothesis: public spaces in Juchitán should function as alternate water management infrastructure as well as resilient spaces that are prototypes of efficient and sustainable construction systems. The plan for CRI Hidalgo includes an outdoor cistern that collects rainwater, which is then filtered into an underground water storage. Outside of the rainy season the space can be used as a playground as well as an auditorium, with the brick steps that separate the cistern area from the basketball court functioning as seating. For teenagers, there is a small

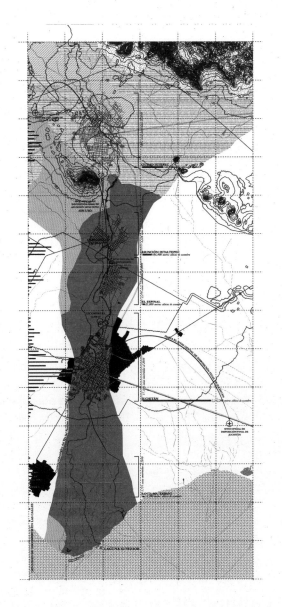

Map and drawing of the towns along Los Perros
River, the debris caused by the September 2017
earthquakes, and the locations where the debris
was deposited.

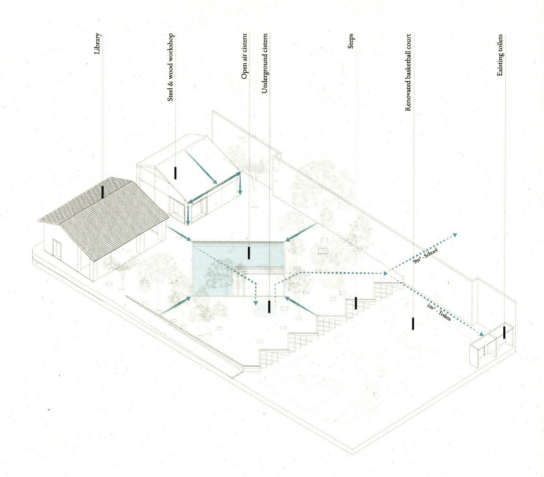

Library

Steel & wood workshop

Open air cistern

Underground cistern

Steps

Renovated basketball court

Existing toilets

9m³ - School

1m³ - Toilets

The new steel and wood workshop follows
the volume of the adjacent library.
The project focuses on harvesting rainwater
underground for later use in
schools and toilets.

wood and steel workshop and a fifty-square-meter graffiti wall.

Is it possible to use debris to construct CRI Hidalgo? The city of Lisbon was completely rebuilt after the devastation of the 1755 earthquake and fire through a system called *gaiola pombalina* that reused debris instead of discarding it.[1] In the case of Juchitán, bricks and material from collapsed buildings are usually dumped in the street to be thrown away. The project focuses on using this debris for the reconstruction. Architecture is materialized under the principle of reuse: bricks for the ground and building and pavement debris for wall construction. The project also upgrades the role of public spaces during natural disasters. Throughout the year CRI Hidalgo holds daily activities for children and teenagers and serves as a shelter for humans and goods during times of disaster thanks to both the workshop and the library.

The design of the open-air cistern, steps, playground, and vegetation is based on the geometry of traditional isthmian embroidery. Part of the materialization of this layer consists in the recovery of bricks from the thousands of buildings that were damaged or collapsed in the earthquakes. The ground is elevated fifty centimeters so that it is level with the planters that occupy most of the park. This eliminates borders between street and public space and also helps generate slopes within the public space to collect rainwater from roofs and the ground. Broad ramps provide easier access to the site.

The workshop is a square-floor-plan building, designed following the massification techniques of Juchitán's traditional constructions, in particular the one that houses a children's library. Sixty-centimeter-thick walls follow the *gaiola pombalina* system: a rigid steel-frame structure, later filled with debris, structures the construction, and is covered by a light gable roof. Four large openings in the corners connect the workshop to the public space.

The rigid wooden structure of the *gaiola pombalino* system in a building in Lisbon is filled with debris.

## Brick recovered and stored for later use during the post-earthquake period in Juchitán.

1   "The *Gaiola* is constituted by a set of plane trusses, called *frontal* walls, connected atthe corners by vertical bars that belong to orthogonal frontal walls. Each frontal wall is constituted by a set of triangles, a geometry similar to the steel trusses of nowadays. Since the triangle is a geometric figure that cannot deform without variation of the length of the sides, in fact it is the only one, each frontal wall only needs to mobilize the axial force of its bars to resist forces in any direction in its own plan. Therefore, the connection between orthogonal frontal walls by means of common vertical wood bars yields a tridimensional truss capable of resisting forces applied in any direction. In general the space between the wood bars of the frontal walls is filled with weak masonry, and the surfaces are covered with a finishing material, therefore the Gaiola in general is not visible." Mário Lopes et al., "Pombalino Constructions: Description and Seismic Assessment," in *Structural Rehabilitation of Old Buildings*, ed. Aníbal Costa, João Miranda Guedes, and Humberto Varum (Berlin: Springer, 2014), 188.

Funding the reconstruction project has not been an easy task, but it is highly rewarding when we as architects are able to set up a successful collaboration between the government, donors, and the community. Taller Capital believes that the architect of the twenty-first century needs to address some of humanity's most compelling problems by fully using the incredible capabilities of design—both traditional and modern, sustainable and future-oriented. The tools of our profession establish the common ground where fruitful dialogues between diverse constituents can become architecture.

# KnitCrete:
# Building in Concrete with a Stay-in-Place Knitted Fabric Formwork

Mariana Popescu, Matthias Rippmann, Tom Van Mele, Philippe Block

Today, advancements in computational design tools have enabled architects to explore intricate geometries with ease. Simultaneously, computer numerically controlled (CNC) machinery has facilitated their fabrication. Together, these developments may give the false impression that any imaginable geometry can be built. They have caused the onset of a paradigm shift from the mass standardization of the 1960s and 1970s to mass customization and fabrication starting in the 1990s. While digital fabrication has opened up new opportunities for the construction of complex and optimized structures, it has yet to address cost and material efficiency in custom concrete construction. Formwork for bespoke geometries can usually not be reused; it is a one-off product and therefore becomes waste after construction. This is a problem both in terms of cost and sustainability.

Designing structures that intelligently include structural performance and architectural geometry leads to beautiful, economical, and structurally optimized systems that use very little material. For example, doubly curved and rib-stiffened surface configurations offer the possibility to increase the load-bearing capabilities of a structure in a materially efficient and economical way. These structures have expressive, intricate, and nonrepetitive geometries. As a result, they can be challenging to build with traditional formwork methods that rely on single-use cut timber or milled foam, moving the problem of labor, cost, and waste from the structure to the mold needed to build it. These custom-milled formwork constructions account for approximately one-half to as much as two-thirds of a structure's cost.[1] Moreover, the placing of reinforcements and the integration of additional functional elements are not trivial for bespoke geometries. Other than the high cost associated with bespoke formworks, traditional fabrication strategies are generally slow, requiring months of carpentry work or CNC milling (>240min/m²).[2] As such, traditional approaches to formwork are economically and ecologically not viable for nonstandard doubly curved and reinforced structures.

To harness the full potential of these structures, the formwork systems used for construction need to be rethought. Moreover, these methods need to reduce embodied energy, waste, labor, and cost while increasing customizability, productivity, and construction times.

In traditional formwork systems, rigid and often heavy molds are held in place by scaffolding, which need foundations, and other temporary elements that make up a falsework (figure a). Using a flexible membrane or fabric instead of a rigid mold can offer an alternative forming system needing minimal or no scaffolding (figure b).

Flexible formwork systems using fabric formwork, such as the one used in the Nest HiLo roof prototype,[3] have proven to reduce the waste and labor traditionally associated with constructing nonstandard geometries in concrete.[4]

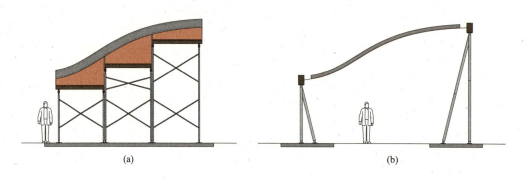

(a)　　　　　　　　　　　　(b)

# Principal representation of rigid and flexible formwork systems: (a) traditional rigid formwork system; (b) flexible formwork system using a textile.

Using weft-knitted textiles within these flexible systems broadens the geometric possibilities and functional integration, and eliminates the need for traditional milled formworks. Moreover, they drastically reduce the need for additional support and scaffolding and simplify on-site logistics.

Knitted textiles are made by the interlocking of a thread to produce a series of loops. These can be produced in various configurations by a versatile CNC manufacturing process using materials that range from natural fibers (cotton, jute, etc.) to technical yarns (carbon, glass, aramid fiber, etc.). The resulting textiles can have varying widths and curved 3-D shapes that conform to predefined geometric and structural needs. Furthermore, in contrast to single-layer woven textiles, they can include features such as channels, holes, spacers, ribs, and so forth, without the need for extensive patterning, cutting, sewing, gluing, or joining several pieces. The produced fabric is foldable; it's easy to pack and transport to the work site. The desired mold is obtained by prestressing the custom-tailored textile in a frame and coating it with a special cement paste. This stay-in-place mold becomes the basis for incredibly efficient, lightweight structures.

Such an approach offers the possibility of creating lightweight deployable systems with tailored material properties that could also be used as reinforcement for the final

KnitCandela waffle shell at the MUAC (Museo Universitario Arte Contemporáneo) in Mexico City.

structure. The latest constructed prototype, KnitCandela, demonstrated the feasibility of using weft-knitted fabrics as stay-in-place formwork for doubly curved concrete geometries at an architectural scale. Using novel computational design methods and KnitCrete formwork, this approach showed that the range of buildable anticlastic geometries can be expanded.

KnitCandela is a thin, undulating, fifty-meter-square concrete waffle shell built at the Museo Universitario Arte Contemporáneo (MUAC) in Mexico City as part of the first exhibition of

241

Zaha Hadid Architects in Latin America in the fall of 2018. The flexible cable-net and knitted-fabric formwork, weighing just 55 kilograms, supported the casting of the five-tonne concrete shell. The final design, developed by the Block Research Group at the Institute for Technology in Architecture, ETH Zurich, in collaboration with the Computational Design Group of Zaha Hadid Architects (ZHCODE), pays homage to the Spanish Mexican shell builder Félix Candela (1910–1997).

Following a digitally generated knitting pattern, the fully shaped, double-layered 3-D knitted shuttering of the formwork was produced in just 36 hours on a commonly available CNC knitting machine and transported to Mexico City inside two pieces of checked luggage.

# Forming the waffle shell: a stiffened textile with inflated pockets (textile 3 cm thick, inflated pockets 4 cm thick)

Tensioned cable-net and knitted-textile
formwork and the minimal scaffolding needed
in comparison to a traditional rigid system.

The load-bearing cable net was integrated
within a custom 3-D knitted textile,
tensioned in a temporary timber frame,
and coated with a special cement paste
that was developed at the Physical
Chemistry of Building Materials chair,

ETH Zurich, to obtain the formwork for
the concrete casting.

Besides channels for guiding the cables,
the textile also features integrated pockets
for fitting and controlling inflatables

forming the cavities of the three-centimeter-thick concrete waffle shell with four-centimeter-high stiffening ribs.

As a thoroughly efficient, ecologically conscious construction system, the stay-in-place mold for this complex structural geometry is practically zero-waste. The minimal foundations and scaffolding required to realize KnitCandela's formwork present a glimpse into how such expressive forms can be realized with a minimal footprint, in record time, and at low cost. The entire design, fabrication, and construction process took 3.5 months, and the formwork, excluding reusable scaffolding, cost only €2,500.

The computationally designed, materially and waste-efficient approach demonstrated in KnitCandela targets all those areas where project timelines and budgets often get out of control: transport and on-site logistics, manual labor, installation costs, and so forth, while also being an elegantly designed structure. The system has the potential to revolutionize construction, from the most mundane structures through to highly customized, fully bespoke buildings. Most importantly, it confronts the challenges faced by the building industry today and in the future, offering practical, easily realizable solutions for a more sustainable way of building.

1   B. García de Soto, Isolda Agustí-Juan, Jens Hunhevicz, Samuel Joss, Konrad Graser, Guillaume Habert, and Bryan T. Adey, "Productivity of Digital Fabrication in Construction: Cost and Time Analysis of a Robotically Built Wall," *Automation in Construction* 92 (December 2017): 297–311.
2   A. Søndergaard, Jelle Feringa, Florin Stan, and Dana Maier, "Robotic Abrasive Wire Cutting of Polymerized Styrene Formwork Systems for Cost-Effective Realization of Topology-Optimized Concrete Structures," *Construction Robotics* 2, nos. 1–4 (2018): 81–92.
3   A. Liew, Y. R. Stürz, S. Guillaume, T. Van Mele, R. S. Smith, and P. Block, "Active Control of a Rod-Net Formwork System Prototype," *Automation in Construction* 96 (2018): 128–40.
4   D. Veenendaal, M. West, and P. Block, "History and Overview of Fabric Formwork: Using Fabrics for Concrete Casting," *Structural Concrete* 12, no. 3 (2011): 164–77.

KnitCandela short credits:
BRG & ZHCODE with R-Ex
– Block Research Group, ETH Zurich (BRG)
– Zaha Hadid Architects Computation and Design Group (ZHCODE)
– Architecture Extrapolated (R-Ex)

# Catch-22:
# Material Needs
# versus
# Material Impact

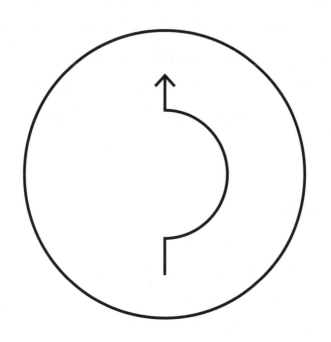

Construction consumes about half of all resources extracted from the earth, and cement production alone accounts for roughly 7 percent of global $CO_2$ emissions. Reducing that environmental footprint will require a new approach to design and construction to decrease our overall use of building supplies. We must find the best materials for the local context rather than simply grafting methods designed for advanced economies onto projects in the developing world, which today accounts for the bulk of consumption. And this all must happen at a cost that is competitive with an industry that has grown hyper-efficient due to the massive volumes it produces.

The good news in those headline numbers, however, is that the immense volumes mean even incremental improvements in performance can have a huge positive impact. In this section, we examine some potential solutions, ranging from increased use of locally available supplies to low carbon cement production to lean designs that don't exceed the requirements of building regulations.

Karen Scrivener
Harry Gugger

# MaGIC:
# Marginal Gains in Construction

John Orr

Construction is a ten-trillion-dollar industry; in creating and maintaining our built environment, it underpins economies and worker productivity. Yet despite its importance, construction sector productivity has been flatlining for decades. Practices that have transformed other sectors, including automation and lean principles, have not yet been adopted.

Limiting temperature rise to 1.5°C will require an 80 percent cut in greenhouse gas emissions by 2050. This is significant for buildings and construction, as these sectors account for 40 percent of energy-related $CO_2$ emissions. We also expect to add 2.5 billion people to our cities by 2050 and 230 billion square meters of new floor space by 2060—with just under half of this occurring in countries without mandatory building energy codes. So in parallel to cutting emissions, we must accommodate a growing, and increasingly urban, population.

To effectively tackle climate change, historic practices of inefficient overdesign must be reversed. Success in reducing the energy required to operate buildings, and the introduction of strict targets for near-zero-energy buildings in Europe, now means that the energy associated with materials can approach 100 percent of total whole-life energy consumption. The importance of this is highlighted by our analysis, which found that embodied energy savings in the order of 50 percent are possible.

The aggregation of small marginal gains that collectively deliver transformations

# Structural optimization of concrete slabs creates new geometries that require new fabrication technologies.

in performance have been successful in health care, aviation, and sport. The approach requires performance measurement, allowing decisions to be made with certainty. Today, the design of buildings is done under a cloud of uncertainty—we don't know what loads the building will be subject to, or how it will respond to them. Simulations at the design stage use arbitrary partial safety factors and confidence intervals, and experienced designers add their own sleep-at-night factors, consuming material as a risk mitigation strategy. If we are to improve performance, then measurement, reporting, and learning must become the key tenets upon which design is based.

Marginal Gains in Construction (MaGIC) brings together multiple programs of work that examine mainstream construction, rather than its glamorous extremes, to achieve maximum impact: Enough Is Enough targets lean design, Automating Concrete Construction (ACORN) examines robotics, the Get It Right Initiative (GIRI) targets the root causes of errors, and Minimising Energy in Construction (MEICON) addresses material efficiency and design culture.

In 2017, MEICON surveyed structural-engineering practitioners to "examine culture and practice […] as it relates to embodied energy." We revealed wide variations and uncertainty in both regulated and cultural behaviors. We found that embodied energy efficiency is not yet a high design priority, resulting in buildings that consume more of our resources than necessary.

MEICON found that individuals do not want to waste material. However, they allow potential future construction errors to influence sizing decisions, simplify designs to improve constructability, and work in teams that do not require embodied energy to be minimized. The incentives of clients, architects, engineers, legislators, and contractors are not yet sufficiently aligned to make minimum whole-life embodied energy the preferred outcome. As a result, material savings of 50 percent are routinely overlooked.

GIRI looks at project practice in order to assess how errors that cost money and material can be avoided. It has found that around 21 percent of UK construction costs (£21 billion per year) are due to errors. This waste has a value some seven times greater than the annual profit of the sector. The causes were found to be rooted in

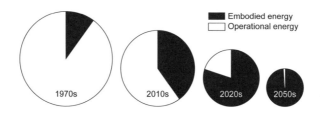

The increasing importance of embodied energy compared to operational energy consumption (approximate data for the UK built environment).

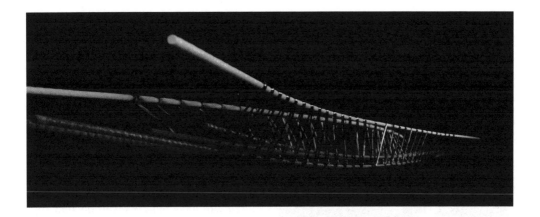

# Carbon-fiber reinforcement cage for a concrete beam fabricated using robotics.

inadequate planning, late design changes, poor communication, and poor culture in relation to quality. The evidence from GIRI suggests that high levels of project-management activity alone are not enough, and that broader change is required to move from a culture of "get it done" to "get it right." This will require new skills and management processes that support improved construction technologies and techniques.

Construction is both labor intensive and highly fragmented: 94 percent of construction companies in Europe have fewer than nine staff members. Construction sites are also heavily influenced by historic practices—the sector only ranks above agriculture in its level of digitization, and change is

slow. A key component in transforming construction will be the implementation of end-to-end processes that link design decisions to component fabrication and building assembly and can embed within each stage an assessment of whole-life performance. Automating Concrete Construction (ACORN) looks to achieve this through mass customization. By using appropriate automation to design out errors and waste and embed sensing to facilitate performance measurement, ACORN aims to meet the productivity and cost savings associated with mass production without constraining design freedom.

Lean design applied to buildings has the potential to reduce not just carbon dioxide but also costs. Enough Is Enough has identified £3.7 billion in potential savings

for the United Kingdom by shaping structures to resist the loads applied to them and no more. Simply adding "and no more" to design codes and procurement documents could have significant benefits. Not only do overdesigned structures emit more carbon dioxide than necessary, they require more deliveries, meaning more air pollution and traffic accidents. Changing processes to put material efficiency and positive social impacts at the heart of design will have benefits well beyond any single project.

MaGIC thinking demonstrates how small changes can make a big difference. Cutting cement production in China by just 10 percent would have a bigger effect on global $CO_2$ emissions than ceasing cement production in all of Europe. Such low-hanging fruit are found on a pathway toward being "more good" and not just "less bad," recognizing that time is of the essence and change is required now.

Changing to performance-led design could mean 30 percent fewer concrete trucks, reducing bronchial health problems from pollution in our cities.

# From India: Three Lessons in Sustainable Construction

Soumen Maity

India is witnessing strong economic growth driven by its increasing population, expanding industry, and rapid urbanization. While per capita consumption of building materials is low compared to the rest of the world, cement and brick producers are India's biggest consumers of natural resources and significant contributors to $CO_2$ emissions. Those considerations spurred the Society for Technology & Action for Rural Advancement (TARA), a three-decade-old social enterprise based in New Delhi, to develop greener technologies and processes for the construction industry. Three of these—EcoKilns, Limestone Calcined Clay Cement (LC3), and new methods for the reuse of construction waste—have been proven at commercial scale and are being adopted by companies small and large.

The EcoKiln, developed in India and now being promoted in several African countries, offers a more energy-efficient way of creating burnt-clay bricks. The EcoKiln consists of a rectangular shaft lined with a heat-resistant refractory surface. After workers load dried green bricks and a measured amount of fuel from the top, the bricks are heated and hardened before being unloaded from the bottom. This technique can reduce emissions and improve the quality of the bricks, with consistent durability and uniform color, shape, and size. Traditional brick production relies on fuelwood, but the EcoKiln can use coal or biomass briquettes, and unlike most kilns, it has a roof that protects it from rain. That allows it to operate year-round, even in the rainy season, providing secure employment to local workers. The modular way the kiln

Brick production
technologies are
followed across Africa.

China clay waste
is used as a raw
material in LC3.

The EcoKiln
technology has been
adopted in Malawi,
Africa.

Building entirely made
out of LC3 in India.

Unsegregated C&D waste in India.

High-quality building material produced from processed C&D waste.

is put together means it can be expanded as demand increases. With the right selection of soil and good brickmaking practices it reduces breakage, and its operational costs are roughly 15 to 30 percent less than traditional methods.

One of every twenty tons of man-made carbon dioxide that enters the atmosphere comes from cement-plant kilns. To help meet growing demand while reducing $CO_2$ output, TARA teamed up with EPFL in Switzerland as well as IIT Delhi and IIT Madras in India to develop a low-carbon cement that we call LC3. The technology tested by big producers such as JK Lakshmi Cements and LafargeHolcim substitutes a portion of "clinker" with calcined clay, reducing fuel consumption because the clay can be processed at 800°C, significantly less than the 1,450°C needed for clinker. At the same time, it cuts out the carbon dioxide produced during the breakdown of limestone in clinker production. Calcined clay is often dumped as an unusable by-product of china-clay mines, and the crushed limestone we use is waste material from the existing cement industry. LC3 consists of about 50 percent clinker, 30 percent calcined clay, 15 percent crushed limestone, and 5 percent gypsum—which means that almost half of the input is material that had previously been discarded. Making LC3 produces about 30 percent less carbon dioxide than the manufacture of ordinary portland cement.

India produces more than 700 million tons of construction and demolition (C&D) waste annually, most of which is either dumped or used as landfill. TARA has worked with private and government agencies to develop ways to utilize the waste in construction, which can reduce consumption of increasingly scarce natural resources such as sand and aggregate. TARA has demonstrated that efficient management of this rubble can spawn profitable recycling programs, and these have been adopted in public-private partnerships in five cities across India. The waste is segregated, processed, and utilized in creating new building materials, demonstrating the viability of a circular economy at both large and small scales. While reuse and recycling are often dismissed as a pipe dream, they can be profitable even as they preserve our precious natural resources.

TARA's own headquarters in New Delhi illustrates these methods and sets an example of energy-efficient construction. Built in 2009, the building is one of the first in India that aims at zero emissions by balancing technology with tradition. The building has a ferrocement shell and shallow masonry domes, which significantly reduces the use of steel. The building's bricks were made of earth excavated from the site and fly ash from local thermal power plants as well as recycled material from the structure it replaced. Its passive heating and cooling systems can reduce its energy consumption by 40 percent. Water use is minimized via water-conserving faucets and showers, and all of the building's water is recycled.

# Cement and Concrete Materials Science and Engineering Education in Africa: Opportunities for Development

Yunus Ballim

The African continent presents a wide variety of human development needs, and it would be unrealistic to generalize solutions. However, to varying degrees, they all share the persistent underdevelopment "pathologies" referred to by Ali Mazrui: technological lag, poor distribution of wealth along race and class lines, and a fragmented economy characterized by a rich and well-endowed continent with many poor communities.[1] That said, in this early stage of growing demand for infrastructure materials, there is the opportunity to utilize new urban and structural design approaches—ones that include environmental sustainability. This will require an assessment of the development needs throughout the continent, a review of the foundational principles that guide our approaches in responding to development needs, and, importantly, educating students in built-environment disciplines to be sensitive to the contestation between the human need for development and environmental sustainability.

## The Changing Political Landscape in Africa and Its Implications

Taken from the website *Our World in Data*, the figure on the next page maps the changing political landscape of countries around the world over a one-generation period, from 1985 to 2015. Putting aside the inherent difficulties in political categorization, the figure shows a significant change in the political environment in almost all countries on the African continent—toward increased democratic processes. This change seems

257

Political Regime, 1985

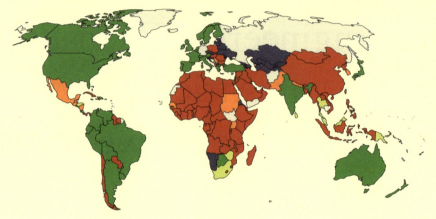

Political Regime, 2015

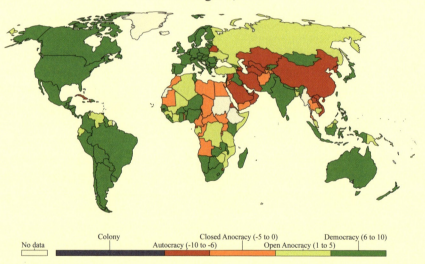

The scale goes from -10 (full autocracy) to 10 (full democracy). Anocracies are those scoring between -5 and 5. "Colony" (coded as -20) includes not only colonies but also countries that were not yet sovereign states (e.g., the Czech Republic and Slovakia from 1945 to 1992).
Source: Political Regime (OWID based on Polity IV and Wimmer & Min)

# Changing political regimes around the world over a thirty-year period.

to indicate that the time of the "big man" African leader is passing, and it may be safe to say that citizens of African countries are learning to better live with themselves in what Achille Mbembe describes as the "postcolony."[2]

This shift in the meaning and agency of citizenship brings both the demand for and the opportunity of delivering on the promise of access to a dignified life. This is a life in which access to basic necessities, such as food, clean water, shelter, health care, and schooling, are guaranteed by society and with acceptable levels of risk of failure. Moreover, this shift means that social institutions are likely to focus on matters of access to social justice by citizens. In the context of the present discussion, this means more housing, hospitals, schools, and roads. But as this development takes place, it is important to consider the ways in which we retain concepts of human dignity as a central value in mediating the allocation of state resources in response to contending social priorities.[3]

Infrastructure Materials Demand and Utilization

There is already evidence that the demand for infrastructure materials is increasing throughout Africa. Reports indicate that from 2014 to 2019 demand for cement in Africa and the Middle East grew at an annual rate of 5.5 percent,[4] the highest in the world. Ethiopia is also predicted to become the fastest-growing country in the world over the next three years, and the government of Kenya has earmarked $55.6 billion for infrastructure development.[5] It is clear that, as the pace of large concrete infrastructure development has slowed in Europe and North America, the center of activity shifted eastward (India, Southeast Asia, and China) and is now showing signs of growth in a number of sub-Saharan countries.

This raises the question as to how such demand can be met without replicating the unsustainable approaches used in other parts of the world. While traditional factors like economic efficiency and technical suitability must remain important in the selection and utilization of materials, African countries have the potential advantage of drawing on the lessons learned in other countries with regard to the environmental consequences of infrastructure-materials usage, ensuring a more sustainable approach to social and economic development. This includes additional factors such as opportunities for reuse, alternative local materials that offer $CO_2$ reduction, and climate-sensitive architectural design and urban planning.

The Role of Materials Science and Engineering Education

Higher-education programs in the area of infrastructure materials should aim to develop a curriculum that is responsive to the tensions between social development and environmental sustainability. For example, in South Africa, corrugated fiber-cement roof sheeting is associated with inferior-quality apartheid housing for poor black communities. This stigmatization was made worse by the presence of asbestos. However, despite the removal of asbestos fibers from production, a general aversion to such material remains. Infrastructure materials also carry social-class markers: the schools of the wealthy are built with clay brick; those of poorer communities are built with easily damaged hollow blocks. There is a "sociology" of infrastructure materials, and the curriculum should aim to develop a sensitivity to these issues in our students.

There is also a need to stimulate university-based postgraduate and research activities in areas that consider the effective and sustainable usage of materials for infrastructure development on the continent. This is necessary to provide the evidence base for development of policy and regulation for more locally appropriate materials utilization. However, most universities on the continent are yet to recover from decades of underfunding and loss of local intellectual capacity. This will require significant investment in laboratory and testing facilities in African universities as well as attracting high-level teaching and research academics in order to be able to provide supervision for students in areas such as structural

efficiency, alternative materials, and durability. Beyond this, researchers must also foster engagement with the infrastructure-materials industry to ensure that the research findings are properly communicated to positively influence design and construction practice.

Lastly, many African countries rely on design and construction codes of practice from regions where conditions are very different, and as a result the infrastructure often shows poor durability or serviceability performance. A particular focus on quality management in design and construction is necessary to reduce the margins needed for safety and improve the material efficiency of structures. Codes of practice must be structured to positively influence sustainable approaches in materials utilization. In developing such codes of practice in countries across the continent, there may well be value in drawing on the framework used in the development of multicountry codes of practice, such as those in Europe.

1 Ali Mazrui, *The African Condition: The Reith Lectures* (London: Heinemann, 1980).
2 Achille Mbembe, *On the Postcolony* (Johannesburg: Wits University Press, 2015).
3 The word "value" refers to that which regulates behavior in the absence of rules—or when the rules cannot be applied.
4 Joseph Green, "Global Demand for Cement to Reach 5.2 Billion Tons," *World Cement*, August 27, 2015, https://www.worldcement.com /europe-cis/27082015/global-demand-cement -billion-tons- 449/.
5 "Rising Cement Consumption Spells Out Growth for East Africa," *Concrete Trends*, October 6, 2015, https://www.concretetrends.co.za/news /rising-cement-consumption-spells-growth-for -east-africa/.

# Concrete as a Socio-technical Process

Elise Berodier

Concrete is now universal. With six billion tons manufactured per year, it is the most used construction material in the world. But this glorious picture of urbanization may have obscured the complex and dual impact of concrete. While concrete continues to provide infrastructure and housing for billions of people, it has transformed our natural environment beyond the point of repair. Current cement production is associated with 8.6 percent of global anthropogenic $CO_2$ emissions. And in certain regions of the world, the scarcity of the natural materials used in concrete, including sand, aggregates, and water, has become alarming. Today, not only is urbanization not pairing with economic growth, but our current construction practices are threating human life. It is therefore urgent to rethink concrete and its production.

More than 90 percent of the carbon dioxide produced by cement occurs during production. The process requires the calcination of limestone at 1,500°C; under such temperature, limestone, a calcium carbonate, chemically decomposes into calcium oxide to form ordinary cement and at the same time releases $CO_2$ gas. One kilogram of cement produces more than half a kilogram of carbon dioxide. The most common solutions are alternative materials to minimize ordinary cement content and an improved calcination process. Other technologies are under consideration; however, while academics and industry experts are increasingly focused on the environmental and economic value of new technology, less consideration is given to the actual use of concrete and the realities of the end user. Developing sustainable concrete

261

production is complex, and we should not focus solely on the engineering aspects. The social and economic contexts should be embraced in the conversation.

As a material scientist, I want to rethink concrete not as an ordinary structural material but as a complex socio-technical process. This comprehensive

Manual mixing: The dosage of the components measured with buckets according to communication with the supervisor.

approach is even more critical, as most of the concrete produced today is in the developing world, where production is not standardized. Haiti offers a fertile ground to examine the challenges of urbanization faced by low-income countries. A third

of Haitians now live in the capital, Port-au-Prince, a major shift compared to the 1950s, when 90 percent of the population lived in the countryside. To demonstrate how concrete is actually used in the field in urbanizing areas and what the consequences are, we conducted a study in Port-au-Prince in August 2018 with the support of the Laboratoire National des Bâtiment et Travaux Publiques d'Haiti and the Swiss Agency for Development and Cooperation.

The first thing tested was the strength as a proxy for the structural quality of the concrete. Fresh concrete was collected from random active informal construction sites. The preparation of concrete is a simple mix of cement, water, and aggregates. However, to guarantee high-quality concrete, a number of procedural details and practices must be respected. The results of this field collection showed that the mechanical performance of concrete varied greatly. Our study found that behind the poor-quality concrete was the incorrect dosage of water. A change in practice is critical to prevent disasters, such as the 2010 earthquake in Haiti, and it is likely that a similar conclusion is what has driven international organizations and governments to embrace reconstruction by "building back better." However, after eight years of intensive initiatives, our results showed that half of the concrete produced in Haiti today is still of suboptimal quality.

Water is added according to the experience of the *maître-pelle* or at the request of the person placing the concrete in the formwork.

While there were many people in Haiti analyzing the prevalence of poor-quality concrete due to the incorrect dosage of water as a consequence of reducing costs or a lack of equipment, our research demonstrated that the lack of knowledge management on construction sites was the primary determinant. This conclusion came from in-depth analysis of the two kinds of supervisors we observed. One category of supervisors was engineers who usually had a formal civil engineering background. The second category was foremen who had learned their job on-site as apprentices, with no formal civil engineering training. The concrete quality was much higher on sites managed by engineers compared to those where a foreman was the primary supervisor; engineers better estimated and controlled the amount of water, while non-engineers had fewer management skills. Our analysis did not explore all dimensions of the effect of an engineer

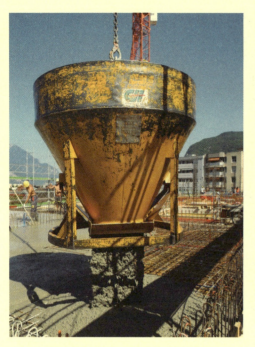

On-site concrete plant: The dosage of the components is controlled precisely in a remote control booth. The composition can be changed via verbal communication by the team working on the slab.

supervising; factors related to the social and economic context could affect the quality, and these factors need to be studied in combination with technical factors to define the right response. Nevertheless, it is clear that formal education is an important element, while equipment and cost are minor.

This then raises the question of whether technology and knowledge are growing adversely. When looking at the Pantheon in Rome, built with comparatively limited technology but still standing today, knowledge appears to be a deciding factor when it comes to the durability of concrete. New construction technologies must grow with the knowledge of the end users and should be robust enough to adapt to the field conditions. If this doesn't happen, the threat to human life will only increase with urbanization, and the case study in Haiti is an illustrative example.

# Urbanism and the Technosphere

Albert Pope

Material Proposition

Approaching the climate problem from the perspective of a single material can be surprisingly productive. We know that living trees sequester carbon and that wood is a highly efficient medium of carbon storage (carbon accounts for 50 percent of its dry weight). Unlike any other material suitable for building at a large scale, forest, trees, and cut wood have an integral role in the planet's carbon cycle. If the ultimate environmental challenge is to bring our carbon-intensive production into equilibrium with that cycle, then to attach this production to part of that cycle's crucial component—urban construction—seems like an obvious place to start.

The specification of a single material in itself, however, is insufficient. A response to climate disruption is not only what material is used in urban construction but how that construction is configured. While the widespread use of wood will reduce emissions, its value will be lost if it is not integrated with the other components of the carbon cycle. This integration requires wood construction to become part of a comprehensive material network called the technosphere.

What makes climate instability such a tricky problem is that the objects and activities that must be reconciled to the carbon cycle are those that are associated with our own survival. Along with the species that inhabit shells, nests, and mounds, humans produce what can be referred to as an "exoskeleton" as a necessary function of our existence. Far more complex than the termite mound, for example, the accumulated human environment is no less integral to our biological survival. Referring to the human exoskeleton as a "technosphere," a 2017 study estimated the weight of the material habitat that humans have created in roads, cities, rural housing, the active soil in cropland, and so forth, at thirty trillion tons, some five orders of magnitude greater than the weight of the human beings that it sustains. That is approximately 4,000 tons of transformed earth for every human being.[1]

In short, humanity is an "infrastructural species," so much so that there is no such thing as a human being apart from the comprehensive networks in which we are always and already embedded. The objects that make up this network are such that they cannot be eliminated without eliminating ourselves, and this is true regardless of how threatening they become to both human and nonhuman life. As a consequence, the now toxic objects of our exoskeleton cannot be eliminated, only transformed through their integration into the natural cycles on which it depends.

Urbanism

How might we legitimately use the word "urbanism" in the context of tons of roads, cities, rural housing? This question raises another: Can the organizational logic of what we call urbanism be used to structure a thirty-trillion-ton technosphere? In North America, this comprehensive infrastructural network emerged from the Land Ordinance Act of 1785 (also known as the Jeffersonian Grid) that lasted up to the middle of the twentieth century. The Land Ordinance Act was an attempt to use an open grid to structure both farmland and township at the scale of the North American continent. That grid-based system broke down midcentury, at the outset of the Great Acceleration, as the forces of industrial capital broke out of the bounds of the traditional agricultural and urban grid. Since that time, agribusiness and mass housing has only accelerated to the point that it seems unlikely they can ever be brought under control again. Given, however, that urban environments count for two-thirds of the world's overall energy consumption and 70 percent of global greenhouse emissions, with agricultural development making up most of the rest, we have no choice but to try to change this.

The traditional logic of urbanism — a traditional, gridded pattern of blocks and streets, farms and fields — would be a proven choice, but it seems unlikely that the thirty-trillion-ton genie that outstripped its gridded logic nearly a century ago can be put back in the bottle. If, however, the technosphere needs to be brought into the carbon cycle, we might well ask what other logic can be

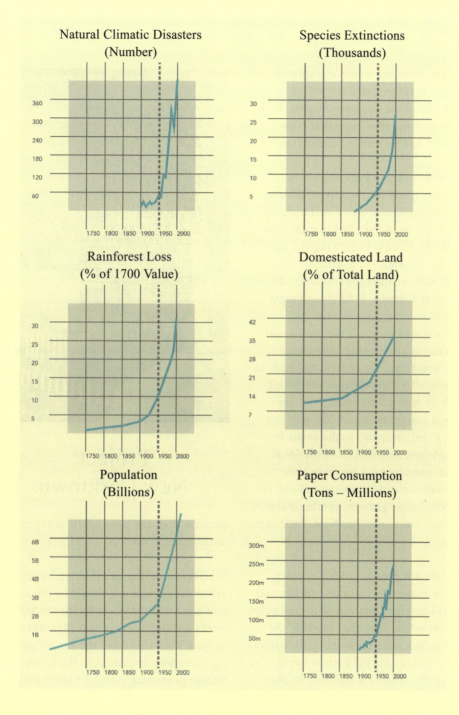

## The Great Acceleration.

used. The short answer is the spine-based urbanism that has come to replace both the urban and the continental grid. This is the organizational logic that New Corktown has set out to demonstrate.

New Corktown is a Present Future project designed for the city of Detroit. The project focuses on a two-block site that was given in the brief, a total project area of 256 blocks. Following the best scientific information available—the United Nations Intergovernmental Panel on Climate Change, Fifth Assessment Report—our response to climate disruption was to reject the traditional urban and environmental response, which, since the late sixties, has been to "think small." This crisis is not small, its effects will not be small, and our response cannot be small. We will not appropriately respond to the crisis by a thoughtless celebration of the local. Instead, our response requires both speed and scale. Attempting to keep up with population growth, another Paris is built each week, another New York each month.

Cities are not permanent but contain complex material cycles and residential cycles. The identification of these cycles is important because they provide the means to integrate urbanism with natural cycles, in this case the carbon cycle. The average life span of a building in the United States is no more than fifty years. This is the upside of cheap American

# Project:
# New Corktown.

construction: the possibility of rapid urban transformation.

When considering an effective model of urban development we must be constantly reminded that the grayest cities in the world are also the greenest. Residents of New York City have the lowest per capita carbon emissions in the United States, generating just 7.1 metric tons of greenhouse gas annually. This is less than 30 percent of the national average, which is 24.5 metric tons per capita annually. In other words, it would require a 70 percent reduction in US per capita greenhouse emissions to reach the emissions level of the average inhabitant of the five boroughs. This reduction is close to the 75 percent reduction in emissions required to limit surface temperatures to a 2°C increase, a limit that was once considered to be manageable. Unknown to most people outside the field, high urban (exoskeleton) densities present a ready-made solution to our environmental problems. Moreover, it is a solution that has been tested and proven many times over.

Cycling Wood into the Technosphere

While neither high-density dwelling nor wood construction alone can have a significant impact, together they would go a long way toward integrating urban production into the carbon cycle. The use of wood in high-density construction is made possible by new technologies that are grouped under the heading of cross-laminated timber (CLT). CLT transforms wood into a sophisticated industrial product capable of satisfying a great number of building requirements, including the construction of high-rises. Cut from the less valuable outer rings of a tree, the layers of CLT panels are composed of relatively small wood sections that would otherwise be milled into wood pellets for fuel or pulped for

particle board or paper products. Despite the fact that the lamination process often reduces wood down to its chemical components (cellulose), it maintains its inherent strength. This strength allows CLT to be used in buildings already fifteen stories high, and has been engineered and tested up to forty stories. Combining CLT construction with high-density urban models, we have succeeded in answering a simple question: How would a city look if it achieved a 75 percent per capita reduction in energy consumption? How would it function? What kind of spaces would we create? What would be its public dimension?

In this proposal, wood is "rendered" in three composite states within the technosphere: wild, cultivated, and processed. The wild state is represented in the riverine systems that abut the redevelopment sites. Instead of promoting a heavily altered riverfront landscape, the projects reimagine the adjacent riverfront park as a restoration or, better, a "rewilding" of the river wetlands, allowing it to resume its integral role in the native ecology. The second state in which wood is rendered in the projects is in a cultivated state. The cultivated state is represented in the extensive carbon plantation bands that run through the redevelopment site. Different from a tree farm or a forest or an urban park, carbon plantations are harvested and replanted on a cycle that is designed to maximize carbon sequestration and storage. Finally, the third state in which wood is rendered is in a processed state. This state, represented by CLT technologies, is used in the fabrication of the project's architectural construction. The wild, cultivated, and processed states in which wood is rendered integrate the project to several separate levels of the carbon cycle. This comprehensive material substrate opens an alternative to building culture that grows out of a reductive set of economic, political, and material objects. From its primitive origins to its most recent technical advances, wood provides a foundation for a comprehensive approach to urban reform. When used to maximum effect, this single material can be of immense value in addressing the climate problems exacerbated by urban construction.

1  See Jan Zalasiewicz, "Scale and Diversity of the Physical Technosphere: A Geological Perspective," *Anthropocene Review* 4, no. 1 (2017): 9–22.

# Building to Cool
# the Climate:
# The New Carbon Architecture

Bruce King

"The primary task of any good teaching is not to answer your questions, but to question your answers."
Adyashanti, *The Way of Liberation*

Imagine

You walk into a brand new building and immediately sense that something is different. The structure is made entirely of exposed wood—the columns, beams, and roof are great curving slabs of timber elegantly joined together. The skin and insulation—which you can also see—are straw, bound into shapes that shield from the rain and insulate the walls. The foundation is soil from the site transformed by invisible microbes into a strong concrete that holds everything up; on top of this are warm, leatherlike floors that need no covering. You think to yourself that it should look and smell like a barn, yet somehow it feels more like an inviting bedroom, or even a museum. It's nicer than any building you've ever been in before.

And it's not a hand-built house in the woods. It's a new downtown office building, nine stories high, full of people and filling half a city block. It gathers all the power and water it needs from the sky, it is elegantly lit by daylight, and it processes all its own water and waste into soil for the courtyard gardens. And, though you can't see it, its construction put thousands of tons less carbon into the air than structures built a decade earlier, and even pulled hundreds more out of the air to serve as the walls, floors, and roof.

But to Back Up a Bit . . .

We've been developing the art of building since the dawn of the agricultural revolution 8,000 years ago. That extended worldwide moment was arguably the most disruptive in history—for us and the rest of life on earth. Rather than hunt and forage for our food, we grew it in one spot, and next thing you know we had architecture, political states, wealth and poverty, global tension, and Wi-Fi-enabled drive-thru hamburger stands everywhere. However, for the last few centuries we've also been learning through science. We now know an awful lot more about how things work than we ever did before, but

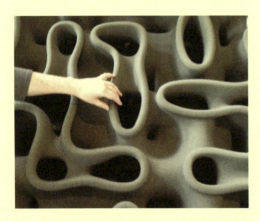

"Sound Wall" made of 3-D-printed rubber by Rael-San Fratello Architects.

we can also dimly see how much we still don't know.

In many ways, the history of architecture follows the development of materials— follows the history of people messing around with things found in the landscape to create bricks, then boards, then toilets, then building-integrated photovoltaic panels. People learned to fire clay to make pottery, and when the kilns were made of limestone they discovered that the intense heat also changed the rocks: lime plaster, concrete, Pantheon. In some places, the potters saw shiny metal oozing out of certain heated rocks: copper, bronze, iron, Golden Gate Bridge. Two hundred years ago engineers in England placed iron bars in the newly invented Portland cement concrete, and architects went wild: the result was every downtown skyline in the world, with lights, plumbing, and comfort hundreds of feet in the air. It seemed like the party would never stop, but the hidden costs are arriving and starting to hurt.

Building materials account for 9 to 15 percent of global emissions, so we have to change not just the way we build, but what we build with. For the past century, it has been increasingly easy and cheap to extract, process, assemble, and transport everything we use in building. Every modern industrial society has codified systems, laws, and standards of construction that are based on abundant fossil fuels and having an "away" where we can throw things—and which even

Wood structure and straw insulation: You can store a lot of carbon in buildings by letting Mother Nature do all the work, harvesting carbon from the sky and turning it into carbon-based structure, insulation, and sheathing. Even though we've been building with trees and plants for 10,000 years, we've only just begun to explore the possibilities of plant-based architecture.

## Straw "Stramit" panels.

anything out of carbon coaxed from the air. The T3, a seven-story office building in Minneapolis, wouldn't be out of place in any North American city, but it's almost entirely wood, with just the ground floor and central core made from concrete. A Lithuanian company called Ecococon and an English company called Modcell offer prefabricated mass timber buildings with integrated straw insulation. A host of companies are creating insulation, wall coverings, and even concrete substitutes from mushrooms and bacteria. Several producers offer "Hempcrete," a mix of hemp (a plant similar to marijuana) and minerals that acts as concrete and insulation. All of these emerging technologies, and more, have arrived in tandem with the understanding that, in the effort to halt and reverse climate change, the embodied carbon of building materials matters more than anyone had thought.

inhibit and penalize those who seek better ways to build. But it won't last much longer: the "heat, beat, and treat" approach to making and processing materials is killing us, as is the notion that we can throw away anything into landfills, water, soil, or the air.

We are in technological reach, within a generation, of creating buildings and cities that generate more energy than they use, reverse the emissions engine, cool the climate, and make nicer places to live and work. It's time to bring the carbon home.

This text is an excerpt from Bruce King, *The New Carbon Architecture* (Gabriola: New Society Publishers, 2007).

Introducing the New Carbon Architecture: Buildings Made of Sky

The built environment can switch from being a problem to a solution. For the first time in history, we can build pretty much

# Standing on a Thin Arch: Incremental versus Radical Change

### Epilogue by
### Simon Upton

As I read the "22 Propositions for Re-materializing Construction," I found myself tempted by seeming opposites. I felt like the countess in Richard Strauss's *Capriccio*—his magical late work that sums up and brings to a close an entire operatic tradition. The countess is pursued by two suitors—a poet and a musician who both press their case in terms of the superiority of their respective craft. Is it the words or the music that are superior? Is it the materials, the physical stuff, or is it the design, the intellectual stuff? Is it bottom-up or top-down? Where ultimately does the solution to our existentially pressing challenges lie?

We find ourselves today on a treadmill of dependency on materials. We are shaped by materials like concrete and steel, which carry with them an incredibly heavy environmental footprint. Concrete alone accounts for 5 percent of global carbon emissions. This is a subset of an even bigger dependency: the energy we rely on to manipulate our constructed world. We — and the places we live in — are shaped by the energy we use.

This is not unique to the world of construction. Think of so-called high-performance sportswear—expensive gear that is perfectly waterproof but breathes. The chemistry is clever, but the environmental fate of the chemical chains is often anything but benign. We may be able to encounter extreme climates with equanimity, but we do so at a cost. We may be able to effortlessly build towers over 300 meters high, but the material needed to do so carries a heavy imprint.

Does a world of clever materials science, especially biomaterials such as mycelium or bio-mineralization, hold the answer? Perhaps, but as designer Phil Ross explains, there is no overwhelming demand for green materials. So if the demand isn't there, we have to look at the way spaces and institutions are designed.

We want to believe what we see. As it is easier
to see a structure than its consequences,
we generally do not see its emissions.
Thus, warning about the risks posed by
something invisible might not be very
compelling. Environmentally, we are all
standing on a thin arch; we will only "see" the
consequences if it collapses.

Eva Pfannes shows us how managing water as a resource means rewiring natural dynamics. Christoph Küffer gives an account of wild design: not just thinking about how things fit together, but radically changing the principles of design to insist that they follow from the environment and its ecosystems, rather than have the environment follow our demands. It's a question of "designing with what you have on hand."

This strikes an immediate chord with Anne Lacaton's brilliant approach to the material use of "make do": improving and never destroying what you have, and in extreme cases, getting upstream of the client and the brief to see if anything needs to be done, to the point of offering nothing material as a solution to a perceived problem!

But there are plenty of people around the world who have nothing other than their degraded environment to work with. Asking them to "make do" with what is clearly inadequate will not suffice. We will have to mobilize resources and build stuff—which brings us immediately to a second key tension: Do any proposed solutions have the required scale, and do we have the time to implement them?

Global population today stands at 7.6 billion; by 2050 it will be ten billion. Instead of mobilizing forty billion tons of material per annum, as we do now, we will be mobilizing ninety billion tons per annum in 2050. Facing this runaway growth, one may argue that there isn't any time available for the costly and disruptive rewiring of our systems and materials. But the planet won't give us much time if we don't. At the current rate of fossil-fuel use, the absolute limit of the emissions budget available—to give us a 50 percent chance of staying within 1.5°C—will last us less than ten years. For a 50 percent chance of staying under 2°C, we have less than thirty years. In both cases, we would need to be at zero emissions—any residual emissions would need to be permanently sequestered. Planting trees is not an adequate substitute.

How, with this little time, do we tackle a problem of such scale? Anne Lacaton is surely right in insisting that we do — when there is something with which we can make do. But the pressure is to provide services where there aren't any and to provide better ones where there are. So, can we intelligently re-materialize?

That brings me to a third tension: Who is in the driver's seat — the person who lives in constructed spaces or the architect and adviser, the intellectual? Everyone seems to agree that the best advocacy starts with listening to the needs of those on whose behalf you act. This is what Laila Iskandar did when she was Egypt's minister of urban renewal and informal settlements, and she gives us an insight into the embedded knowledge of informal waste collectors in Cairo.

Which drives us back to systems: Whether they are spatial or economic, who is the client? For whom are we advocating? Ultimately it is political will that is needed — and that is lacking. And I speak as a former politician who today serves my country's politicians in an independent environmental watchdog role. Politicians will go as far and as fast as people will let them, and they are only as good as their advocacy. I expect they are no better than architects at explaining complexity, but that is what they have to do. They are asked to oversee a mind-bendingly complex social and economic system. Politicians need to be empowered to explain what needs to happen—if architects can't simplify this incredibly complex transformation of an entire economic paradigm or ecosystem, then why should they be able to?

For businesses—and advisers— it means being earnest about problems. They need to find a way to communicate two systemic issues: one environmental, the other economic and social. Environmentally, the issue that needs to be explained is the limit to the planet's ability to absorb our waste. When we were less than a billion and largely rural, we knew the local limits. But now we have to know the global ones. Ultimately it is about waste—of which carbon dioxide is a huge but by no means the only fraction. Eliminating waste from the combustion of fossil fuels—which is largely about eliminating fossil fuels themselves—is a preeminent challenge. And this and other externalities cannot, from what I can see, be tackled without their costs being sheeted home to consumers by prices or, less transparently, by regulations.

The social and economic issue concerns the responsiveness of finance and investment to materials and infrastructures that are compatible with the planet's capacity to absorb waste. It comes down to the interests of those on whose behalf funds are invested. There are hundreds of millions of people whose money — be it through pension savings or health or insurance premiums — is invested by people who do not yet seriously understand their fiduciary duty to invest in a world that will still be livable. This is changing, but slowly. Some European reinsurers and institutional investors are taking these issues seriously. But for the rest, the relentless search for returns in the short term is piling up infrastructure that will remove options in the long term. In many cases, the misalignment in investment reflects real knowledge gaps. Often obsolete technologies continue to be deployed because they come as turnkey solutions that omit vital information about the very causes that could cause the arch of our civilization to collapse.

Both architects and politicians need to be honest about what we do not know. There is a lot of green optimism and green incrementalism out there, but there will be transitional costs. Those who can afford to bear those costs will have to bear them. Those who need to be protected must be protected. It needs to be a just transition, but it will never happen if politicians constantly try to pretend that it is costless. Costs are unavoidable. Either we impose them on our terms, as fairly as we can *ex ante*, or nature will impose them *ex post*. The latter path is unlikely to be socially optimal. Imposing costs today is our way of demanding a future for our children and grandchildren.

Architects, engineers, and responsible businesses can help politicians by proving and demonstrating the technologies, business models, and materials that make a transition possible and bearable. They can help governments link up the key players who will form new value chains. They can help governments undo the regulatory wiring of yesterday's economy. They can fill knowledge gaps by bringing researchers together.

Choosing materials (words for Strauss) is choosing the energy required to produce materials. Transforming energy for power generation and mobility is well on the way. That leaves the hard cases—including steel and cement. Transforming these materials and their energy requirements won't happen through prices alone. It will require a great deal of R&D and material substitution. Plenty of people are working on this already.

What about design (the music), in particular the design of institutional, regulatory, and economic structures? If it is political will — or political education — that is lacking, why not bring together real materials and design expertise with political leaders? We must ensure that we engage with materials and design, the words and the music. The intellectual demands of the challenges we face are enormous. But solutions must be rooted in the economic and social world of the users.

# A Collection of Building Components and Materials

Compiled by
Something Fantastic

Across the building industry, people are becoming increasingly aware of the environmental toll of their work. And yet despite this growing sense of urgency, the shift away from "business as usual" and toward more sustainable standards can seem frustratingly slow.

To help ignite the debate and fire up imaginations, we present this collection of materials—a catalog, if you will—that could be considered a road map to a new, greener future. Many of them may not appear revolutionary or even unusual. Some are widely used. But taken together, they can contribute to a new palette of materials and methods for those who want to build in a better way. We are not advocating a radical shift in architecture or principles of construction but rather seeking to raise awareness of sustainable practices that waste less energy and space—and that don't consume natural resources beyond their capacity to regenerate.

This palette is as broad as it is varied. It includes locally sourced materials (p. 322), materials from natural, renewable sources (p. 307), and minimally processed materials (p. 296). It can lead us to greater sustainability by saving space (p. 380) or supplies (p. 306). It can increase efficiency by opening buildings up rather than sealing them off from the environment (p. 294) or by incorporating materials found at building sites (p. 292).

The good news here is that the scale of the environmental threat posed by construction means that even small steps can play an outsize role in saving the planet. Few of the materials or products presented in the following pages are in themselves sustainable, but when applied intelligently, they can help us build in a more sustainable way. Not in the distant future, but right now.

# Use What's Already There: Lime-and-cement-based mortar can be mixed with local aggregates

Building sites are notoriously messy, littered with rubble and supplies left over from previous construction projects. At this Spanish location, an adjacent road had to be widened, so the perimeter wall was demolished. The architects decided to incorporate the rubble from that wall into the new structure, using its profile to inspire the home they were building. An important element was adapting local mortar recipes to allow for the upcycling of resources that were already on-site—reducing the need to haul away waste and bring in new supplies.

Example: House 1413, Ullastret, Spain

Contributed by: Harquitectes, Spain

# Expand Your Horizons:
## A simple way to improve insulation and extend living space

Movable walls and windows that can be adjusted by users offer a smart path to flexible, energy-efficient, and affordable design. A robust, inexpensive sliding door can help create environments adaptable to inhabitants' needs. Rooms can be enlarged or divided. Interiors can extend to the exterior. Layouts can be changed according to the weather or simply an individual's whims—allowing for creative and enjoyable use of space.

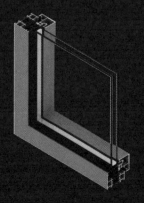

Example: Sliding Wall Tigal by Technal®,
seen in Tour Bois le Prêtre, Paris, by Druot,
Lacaton & Vassal

Contributed by: Lacaton & Vassal, France

# An Ur-material Reconsidered: Prefabrication can modernize a traditional building method

The ancient technique of building with rammed earth offers advantages such as the material's moisture storage capacity, which buffers humidity in a room, and a high thermal mass that eases swings in temperature. Walls are typically created on-site by compressing locally excavated dirt into frameworks. To speed up production, it's possible to adapt existing facilities near the building locale where walls and other elements can be prefabricated in varying shapes and sizes with a mobile ramming machine. After drying, these are transported to the construction site where they are integrated into the structure.

Example: Prefabricated interior rammed-earth wall from Lehm Ton Erde Baukunst, seen in Ricola Herb Centre, Laufen, Switzerland, by Herzog & de Meuron

Contributed by: Martin Rauch, Austria

# Bring On the Bamboo:
# A traditional material serves as
# the basis of an alternative to steel

Natural bamboo is widely used as a building material in equatorial countries. Researchers at the Future Cities Laboratory in Singapore and KIT Karlsruhe have developed processes that promise to give bamboo a renaissance as an industrial product that could replace steel. The bamboo fibers are extracted and then reformulated into sheets and beams for use in construction. The composite material is as strong as steel but lighter and cheaper to produce, and it binds carbon dioxide instead of emitting it.

Example: Bamboo composite material, seen in the Rumah Tambah project, Batam, Indonesia, by Stephen Cairns, FCL Singapore

Contributed by: Alternative Construction Materials FCL Singapore and Sustainable Construction KIT Karlsruhe, Germany

# Embrace the Rubble:
# Use debris from buildings
# damaged in earthquakes

After a massive earthquake struck Lisbon in
1755, Portuguese engineers developed a robust
reconstruction method, called *gaiola pombalina*,
in which rigid wood structures are filled with
debris gathered from collapsed buildings.
Today, an updated version of this idea is being
proposed for the town of Juchitán in Oaxaca,
devastated by an earthquake in 2017. Instead of
wood, the frames are made from rigid steel and
are filled with material recovered from nearby
buildings—so the rubble won't be dumped into a
nearby river.

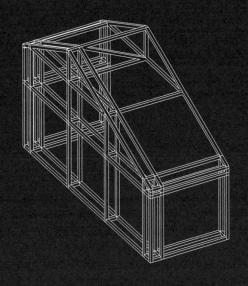

Example: The *gaiola pombalina* system
and building debris, seen in construction in
Juchitán, Mexico

Contributed by: Loreta Castro Reguera and
José Pablo Ambrosi (Taller Capital), Mexico

# Cheap, Recyclable Facades:
When kept separate from other materials, even polymers can be sustainable

A plastic facade wouldn't typically be on anyone's list of sustainable materials. But in certain contexts, these translucent, insulating polycarbonate sheets make sense. The panels are available in various thicknesses, offer thermal insulation similar to that of a brick wall seven times as thick, and are relatively inexpensive. Though they come with a comparably short ten-year warranty, they typically last much longer, which makes them a good fit for low-cost buildings. And since the sheets aren't usually attached to other materials, the polycarbonate can be melted and recycled when it's time to replace the facade.

Example: Nine-chamber Multi Wall Sheets
Rodeca, seen in Brunnenstraße 9, Berlin

Contributed by: Brandlhuber+, Germany

# Air-Freshening Tiles:
# A facade that can improve air quality and brighten the backyard

In a process similar to photosynthesis, the titanium dioxide coating on these tiles produces oxygen when exposed to sunlight and humidity. At the same time, the antifungal surface is hydrophilic and self-washing, which helps cut maintenance costs. And the tiles' glossy finish and angled surface can reflect light into darker spaces such as rear courtyards, as in this residential and studio building by ifau and Heide & von Beckerath.

Example: Hytect tile from Deutsche Steinzeug, seen in the residential and studio building at the former Berlin flower market (IBeB), Berlin

Contributed by: Heide & von Beckerath, Germany

# Minimize the Stuff You Use: Vaulted concrete slabs help reduce overuse of materials

Despite its central role in contemporary building, concrete is frequently applied inefficiently —we use more than is necessary to ensure structural integrity, particularly to span space, for instance in floors. One option would be these structurally optimized concrete floors made with recyclable 3-D-printed molds. The thin, rib-stiffened shell floors can reduce concrete consumption by up to 70 percent and allow use of lower-strength materials that require less carbon to make.

Example: Rib-stiffened funicular floor system

Contributed by: Block Research Group,
ETH Zurich, Switzerland

# A Nineteenth-Century Marvel, Revived: Linoleum is versatile and made from natural, renewable resources

Though linoleum has been around since the 1860s, it's increasingly relevant as we seek to build more sustainably. It's versatile, ages beautifully, and is made from 100 percent natural, renewable resources such as linseed oil, ground cork, wood dust, and jute. It can be laid out continuously to create an uninterrupted floor plane without visible joints, so it's easy to clean and can unify space. And the mid-gray tone 3369 Titanium shown here is bright enough to reflect light but sufficiently dark to appear clean even in heavily trafficked areas.

Example: Forbo Marmoleum® Walton Uni in color 3369 Titanium

Contributed by: Johnston Marklee, USA

# Be Adaptable:
A key to sustainability is an ability to question your own thinking

Sometimes it pays to be flexible and open to changing even long-held plans. When Belgian architect Jan De Vylder arrived at a construction site, a contractor was painting a metal beam green even though the plans specified another color. When De Vylder challenged the painter, he responded that the green was the paint used to protect the metal, and he could add a further coat of any color De Vylder wanted. But in the end De Vylder decided to stick with the green, making it an integral part of the entire design and ultimately using the idea in other projects.

Example: UV-resistant, anti-corrosion paint, seen in House 43, Ghent, Belgium

Contributed by: Jan De Vylder, Inge Vinck; Architecten De Vylder Vinck Taillieu, Belgium

# A Transparent Solution:
# A film that plays with light and keeps the heat out

Privacy film can create opacity, transparency, or reflection, depending on where the light source is located. And adding it to a single-glazed window can double the insulation, making it almost as effective as a double-glazed window at a fraction of the material and monetary cost. By reducing cooling and heating loads, the film can serve as an alternative to installing new windows or HVAC systems in existing buildings.

Example: Privacy film by 3M, seen in Aesop Wynwood, Miami, FL

Contributed by: Frida Escobedo, Mexico

# Invasive Plant, Innovative Aggregate: Removing eucalyptus trees provides employment and a building material

Concrete is usually made by combining cement with aggregates such as sand and gravel. In South Africa, an alternative aggregate is wood chips from invasive species, which offers environmental benefits that go far beyond the building sector. The wood comes from non-native plants, such as eucalyptus trees, that threaten the local flora, consume an outsize share of scarce water resources, and fuel wildfires. Locals are hired to cut the plants and grind them into wood chips, which are then mixed on-site using low-cement binder. The wood-chip formula offers sufficient strength to build multilevel structures and has a three-hour fire rating—triple the level of conventional building materials.

Example: Light House Invasive-wood-chip aggregate, developed by the Department of Environmental Affairs of the Republic of South Africa, South Africa

Contributed by: Stephen Lamb, South Africa

# A Greener Cement:
# LC3 offers a lower-carbon alternative to the key ingredient in concrete

Some 5 percent of man-made carbon dioxide entering the atmosphere comes from the kilns of cement plants. Until someone discovers an alternative, cleaning up the way cement is made will be key to sustainability. Limestone Calcined Clay Cement, or LC3, takes a big step in that direction. The relatively low-tech solution replaces much of the clinker used for traditional cement with heated clay. This reduces fuel consumption because the clay can be processed at around 800°C, about half the temperature needed to produce clinker. And less clinker means burning less limestone, so less carbon is released. The material is slowly becoming available as cement producers worldwide experiment with the idea.

Example: LC3

Contributed by: Soumen Maity, India

# Slow Down and Sip the Lemonade: Citric acid can make mortars easier to work with

Citric acid isn't generally considered a building material, but it can help make other materials more useful. When added to fast-setting mortar, the acid slows the process of setting, giving builders a few extra minutes to work with the material and, if necessary, make corrections. This avoids mistakes that lead to replacements and waste, and it allows a wider circle of users such as semiprofessionals or laymen to use a high-performance material in a sustainable way. And when the workers get thirsty, the leftovers can be turned into lemonade.

Example: Food-grade fruit acid $C_6H_8O_7$, seen in facade reconstruction of Dieskaustraße 101, Leipzig, Germany

Contributed by: Summacumfemmer Architekten, Germany

# Optimize at the Factory: Prefabricated elements help reduce consumption of concrete

While most big building projects rely on concrete poured at the site, prefabricated concrete elements can help dramatically reduce the amount of material that gets used. That's because it's hard to plan and build close to the structurally necessary minimum, so most builders simply use too much stuff. Prefabricated elements, by contrast, can more easily be optimized to meet a project's true structural needs, especially for low-cost buildings. They use less concrete, so they're lighter. And because they're easy to install they allow for tight, reliable scheduling. The product presented here is just one example. Similar materials are available almost everywhere, and the closer the producer is situated to the building, the more efficient their use.

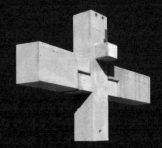

Example: Prefabricated structural concrete elements from Allton/HV Fertigteile, seen in Waldenserstraße 25, Berlin

Contributed by: FAR frohn&rojas, Germany

# Building with Boulders:
# Use stones excavated from a site
# to connect a structure to its locale

It's not unusual to find rocks and even boulders lurking just beneath the surface of construction sites. These are typically hauled away at great expense, but here's a better idea: use them in your project. This one was placed above the fireplace in a private home, where its unique texture and shape offer a reference to the history of the site while balancing temperature swings with its great thermal mass. And as a nonprocessed, locally sourced raw material, its environmental impact is minimal.

Example: Excavated boulder seen in the mantelpiece of a private home in Malveira da Serra, Portugal

Contributed by: José Forjaz, Mozambique

# Love Your Local Quarry:
# Stone walls rather than veneers offer a durable, weather-resistant facade

A natural-stone facade can show an architect's appreciation and respect for a cultural or political institution while embracing the traditions and architectural heritage of a place. These days, that often means applying a thin layer of stone that was mined far away and attached to a contemporary, high-performing facade. But a thick, load-bearing, and structurally independent wall of stones sourced from a local quarry that has been in business for centuries, which can be maintained, replaced, and even reused, is in some cases the better choice.

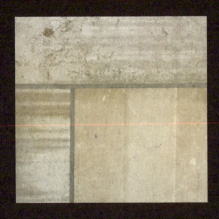

Example: Jurassic limestone, seen in
Kunsthaus Zürich, Switzerland

Contributed by: David Chipperfield Architects
Berlin, Germany

# Don't Forget the Leftovers:
# Stone floors made out of bits and pieces create beauty—and jobs

Using waste is doubly good: it prevents the waste from becoming waste, and using it means you don't need to consume new materials. In the 1920s, terrazzo floors made from leftover rocks from quarries became a common, cheaper alternative to stone floors. While they've become one of the most expensive flooring choices in Europe and the United States, in developing countries with high unemployment terrazzo is a viable option that creates jobs.

Example: Stone leftovers from the local quarry, seen in Avasara Academy, Pune, India

Contributed by: Case Design, India

# Overhead Steel:
# Roof panels can cover wide areas while keeping the spaces beneath cool

Industrially produced steel roof panels are robust, material-efficient, and easy to install. They feature a standing seam, which forms a waterproof connection to the next sheet and allows for the coverage of very large surfaces while creating an appealing, regular pattern. They are available in lengths up to fourteen meters and come in more than twenty standard colors. If chosen in bright white the panels have the additional benefit of reflecting sunlight, which helps keep the surface of the panel up to 24°C cooler than dark roofs.

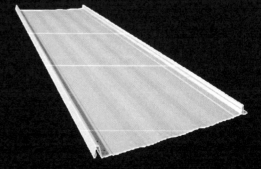

Example: Ameri-Standing Seam Panel (12")
from American Roofing Products

Contributed by: Productora, Mexico

# A Powerful Facade:
# Ultra-thin solar panels can heat water and generate electricity

By combining photovoltaic cells and water-bearing capillaries, this panel produces electricity and heat from sunlight. Both technologies have been successfully used before, on their own and in combination. What distinguishes these panels is their svelte profile—they're just 2.2 millimeters thick—and minimal weight. They can be used in renovations or new construction, creating a power-generating curtain layer in front of a building's facade.

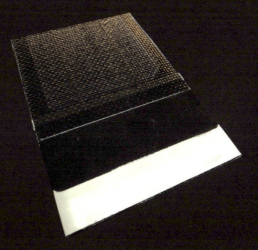

Example: Ultra-thin photovoltaic-thermal collector developed by Architecture and Building Systems Group, ETH Zurich

Contributed by: Arno Schlueter, Switzerland

# Making Timber Great Again: Laminated wood can be an economical choice even for mainstream projects

Laminated wood panels combine the superior qualities of timber—low weight, flexibility, and strength—with characteristics typically lacking in wood: evenness, availability in large formats, and resistance to moisture. They're easy to process and install, and the wide choice of colors and textures makes them an interesting, budget-friendly finishing even in projects that don't look like typical "eco-architecture."

Example: "Maxplatte" laminated wood panels by FunderMax, seen in Torstraße 84, Berlin

Contributed by: Kuehn Malvezzi Architects, Germany

# Bring the Outside In:
# A traditional exterior treatment
# is adapted for interior use

Ceramic bricks are a common feature of exteriors due to their structural properties, versatility, low price, and beauty. But it's far less common to see them on indoor walls, in part due to questions of where to put power and water lines and how to integrate structural elements such as steel supports. Hollow bricks like this one are a simple yet powerful solution. They allow for the inclusion of all fixings and structural elements, and save material because they're hollow and don't require any further wall finish.

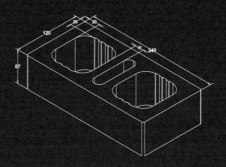

Example: Novaceramic Vintex 6/12, seen in Tello House, Cuernavaca, Mexico

Contributed by: Productora, Mexico

# A Yellower Shade of Pale:
# You don't always need the whitest white to brighten a room

Though RAL 9010 isn't the brightest of the four whites in the RAL palette, its yellow components make it appear brighter than colder tones. This is especially notable when the paint is used in interior spaces without direct sunlight. Brightening such areas can make them more appealing and increase the usable space in a building.

**RAL 9010**

Reinweiß
Pure white
Blanc pur
Blanco puro
Bianco puro
Zuiver wit

Example: RAL 9010, one of 213 colors in the RAL Classic palette, seen in Flottwell Zwei, Berlin

Contributed by: Heide & von Beckerath, Germany

# Reconsidering a Classic Shape: A waterproofing system helped in the construction of light, pitched roofs

The September 2017 earthquake that hit central Mexico sparked an urgent need for lightweight materials that could be quickly deployed and wouldn't stress existing structures that may not have been designed to handle extra weight. One solution was a pitched roof made from reused timber beams and panels, which was covered with a waterproofing film to keep the weight down. This solution provided shelter for people who desperately needed it. And the roof's shape—uncommon in this area—prevents illegal extensions, a major factor in collapsed buildings during earthquakes.

Example: Uniplas Modi waterproofing system by Imperquimia, seen in housing reconstruction in San Gregorio Atlapulco, Xochimilco, Mexico City

Contributed by: Loreta Castro Reguera and José Pablo Ambrosi (Taller Capital), Mexico

# Push Back against the Wind: Adaptivity in structural elements helps reduce material use in buildings

Engineers are taught to anticipate the worst possible load case, so the structural components in most buildings are far stronger than they need to be for the vast majority of situations. A better idea may be to integrate sensors, actuators, and control units into a structure's load path. These can react to external static or dynamic loads to equalize deformations and vibrations—and help reduce the materials needed for a structure by up to 70 percent.

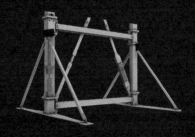

Example: Hydraulic cylinders in columns and bracing elements, developed at ILEK, University of Stuttgart, Germany

Contributed by: Collaborative Research Centre (SFB) 1244, University of Stuttgart

# Strength through Diversity: Using varying kinds of wood in I-beams can boost durability

Laminated wooden beams combine the benefits of wood with those of prefabricated building components. They are available in several sizes and strengths, but they all follow the same principle: the combination of two kinds of wood creates a lightweight, high-performance, low-cost, material-saving component. The central element—the bridge connecting the outer pieces—consists of leftovers from the milling industry. It can be weaker because it typically receives less stress. The two outer flanges are made from sturdier laminated wood to help them bear the beam's load.

Example: Laminated wood IPE beam

Contributed by: Atelier Fanelsa, Germany

# Going Tubular:
## A material used for pipelines in mines is finding broader applications

Giant high-density polyethylene tubes are often used as pipelines for moving wastewater through mines. Their corrugated walls make them extremely sturdy and structurally independent, but they can also be adapted as a structural building material. They happen to be almost 100 percent soundproof, which is insignificant in their original application but offers a host of possibilities for other uses. The pipes were used in a temporary pavilion at Santiago's Museum of Fine Arts, and plans now call for them to be cut in half and incorporated as roof elements in a permanent structure.

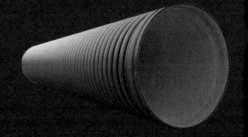

Example: HDPE corrugated structured-wall pipe, seen at the Museum of Fine Arts, Santiago de Chile

Contributed by: Alfredo Thiermann, Chile

# Iron That Grows in the Garden: Untreated bamboo has the strength of steel and, where codes allow, can serve as its replacement

Making steel requires almost fifty times as much energy as growing bamboo, with an equal tensile strength. And bamboo has an impermeable coating that protects it from water, so it won't rot like almost all other organic materials do. Though few building codes allow bamboo as an alternative to steel, there are no restrictions for uses such as these sun shades.

Example: Untreated bamboo rods, seen in Avasara Academy, Pune, India

Contributed by: Case Design, India

# Replacing Walls with Wire: Sustainability can depend on finding smart alternatives

Steel-wire nets aren't necessarily cheap or sustainable. Their cost and material efficiency depends on what they're used for, or more precisely, what they replace. When used instead of concrete, glass, or steel to create a partitioning wall and handrail in a residential staircase, a wire net is a strikingly lightweight and affordable alternative.

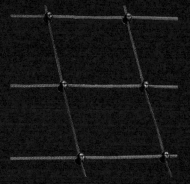

Example: Steel-wire net DRALO from Lothar Huck, seen in Waldenserstraße 25, Berlin

Contributed by: FAR frohn&rojas, Germany

# A Careful Choice of Bricks:
# Using different varieties of brick can cut consumption of materials

Bricks come in a wide range of densities, textures, sizes, and structural characteristics, but most varieties are compatible with one another. That means different kinds can be combined within a building, or even in a single wall, according to varying structural demands. The upper parts of a structure, for instance, aren't as heavy as the lower parts, so the bricks carry a lighter load. Choosing the right bricks for various levels of a wall is a low-tech way of optimizing the use of materials.

Example: Solid brick from Cerámicas Valera, seen in House 1014, Granollers, Spain

Contributed by: Harquitectes, Spain

# Marble Made of Yogurt Pots: A Welsh company produces high-end surfaces from recycled plastics

As long as polymers such as HDPE and PET are sorted and separated, recycling them isn't difficult, but they typically yield fairly humdrum stuff. Smile Plastics in the Welsh city of Swansea has developed a series of materials—each based on a single recycled product—that can serve as countertops, wall coverings, and tiles evocative of high-end natural surfaces such as granite or travertine. The mostly white Alba is made from yogurt pots. Multicolored Kaleido consists of plastic bottles of various hues. Black Dapple, made from chopped-up cutting boards, was used in a bathroom at NEST Dübendorf, where it earned the nickname "Dübendorf Marble."

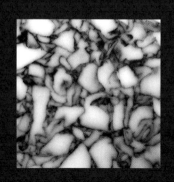

Example: Black Dapple by Smile Plastics, seen in the UMAR unit at Empa NEST in Dübendorf, Switzerland

Contributed by: 2hs Architekten und Ingenieur PartGmbB, Germany

# Multispecies Architecture: Sandblasted wood provides a home—and not just for humans

Sandblasting wood erodes away the soft parts while sparing the harder bits, which creates a rough, ridged surface that highlights the flaws and unique features of lumber rather than erasing them. The result is a "bio-receptive" material that can trap and host microbes, creating a diverse urban microbiome—multi-species architecture, so to speak, that's healthy for humans and the larger ecosystem. The Living used this material in the Embodied Computation Lab at Princeton University, making it not only a lab but also a test case in itself.

Example: Sandblasted wood, developed by The Living, seen in Embodied Computation Lab, Princeton, NJ

Contributed by: David Benjamin (The Living), USA

# White-Line Fever:
# Road paint can replace signs and fences far from the highway

Road-marking paint is extremely robust, withstanding years of traffic, rain, snow, and sunshine. With its various colors and ability to reflect sun and artificial light, it offers a host of design possibilities. While it's not particularly sustainable in itself, those properties mean it can reduce material consumption by replacing certain types of constructed infrastructure such as signs or fences.

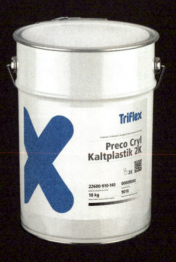

Example: Preco Kryl road-marking paint by Triflex, seen at Berlinische Galerie, Berlin

Contributed by: Kuehn Malvezzi Architects, Germany

# No Need for Cooking:
# A brick that hardens at room temperature

This thin, novel brick draws inspiration from coral, the superhard cement-like material created naturally in the sea. Like coral, bioMason employs natural microorganisms to grow durable cement at room temperature. Sand is mixed into a mold with bacteria, which are fed with a water solution and calcium ions. The bacteria in the bricks creates a cement that requires no baking to harden.

Example: bioLITH by bioMason

Contributed by: David Benjamin (The Living), USA

# Renovate Rather than Raze:
# Adapting older structures is almost always greener than rebuilding

Many structures from the 1960s and 1970s were planned and built with a sort of missionary optimism, but these days they're often reviled by the public and politicians as outdated and ugly. Sure, we could tear them down and replace them, but it would be vastly more sustainable to repurpose and reuse them. We can be inspired by their inventive spirit while updating them to today's standards and adapting them to current needs. The energy, financial, and material cost of renovating is rarely higher than razing and rebuilding.

Contributed by: Muck Petzet Architekten, Germany

# Green Doesn't Have to Be Expensive: Smart use of everyday materials can be an environmentally friendly solution

Sometimes you can get green materials at your local discount store or garden center. Reflective Mylar film—the stuff used in emergency blankets found in first-aid kits—is an extremely light and thin polyester developed by NASA for the exterior surfaces of spacecraft. In the 99¢ Space project—a transformation of a barn that cost less than $1 per square foot—this inexpensive foil was used to create shimmering curtains that double as an insulating layer.

Example: Reflective Mylar film used as a curtain, seen in R3 Ranch, Santa Ynez, USA

Contributed by: Sarah Graham, agps architecture, USA

# The Secret of the Garden:
# Plants can protect a building—and
# provide a habitat for small animals

Incorporating local flora into a structure's design can dramatically increase sustainability. In Europe, leafy vines cool buildings in the summer but allow warming sun to hit a facade in the winter. In this Korean project, bamboo serves as an architectural enclosure redolent of medieval Asian ink paintings. It acts as a sound- and light-buffering screen, ensures privacy, and improves the microclimate via evaporation and shading. And by providing a habitat for birds and other small animals, it eases the strain of urbanization.

Example: Bamboo plantings, seen in Mass Studies HQ, Seoul

Contributed by: Minsuk Cho, South Korea

# No Mortar? No Worries:
# Interlocking bricks can create durable structures from recycled content

Waste-based bricks are rooted in the simple idea that only a small percentage of the ingredients in bricks have to be new clay while the rest can be recycled mineral construction waste. The "UMAR brick" pushes the concept one step further: it has an interlocking system that makes waste-based bricks reusable when a structure is demolished. This means they can be reassembled into walls without mortar or glue. Instead, the bricks are laid "dry" and are post-tensioned by steel rods for structural strength.

Example: Waste-based bricks developed by StoneCycling with KIT Karlsruhe, seen in the UMAR unit at Empa NEST, Dübendorf, Switzerland

Contributed by: 2hs Architekten und Ingenieur PartGmbB, Germany

# Going Green, Hold the Earth Tones: Colorful clay plasters can broaden the appeal of a sustainable material

Clay has a lot going for it: it contains no toxic ingredients, its mass helps buffer swings in humidity and temperature, and it can even filter toxins from the air. But architects have long resisted it, especially in interiors, because it typically came only in various earth tones. This version from Claytec is available in 146 colors based on natural pigments—including white—boosting its appeal far beyond the "green" building community. And when a structure built with clay is razed, the plaster can be recycled simply by dissolving it in water.

Example: White clay plaster Yosima by Claytec, seen in Torfremise, Schechen, Germany

Contributed by: Eike Roswag-Klinge, ZRS Architekten Ingenieure

# From Waste to Walls:
# A Swiss project uncovers
# the beauty of rubble

Construction debris doesn't always have to be ugly. At this Swiss site, broken concrete chunks from nearby teardowns were combined with damaged tiles, bricks, and pavement stones donated by a local landscaper to build walls around a shelter for garbage containers. The rubble was mixed with modest amounts of fresh concrete as binder, and the formworks were removed after half a day so the surface could be washed down to let the beauty of the once-discarded materials show through.

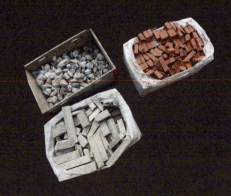

Example: Reclaimed demolition debris, seen in House of Trash, Rotkreuz, Switzerland

Contributed by: AMA, Switzerland

# Cover the Balcony:
## Textile and metal awnings can provide privacy and insulation

Awnings are typically used to protect glass facades from the sun and inclement weather. But placing an awning at the outer perimeter of a balcony can improve insulation while extending living space during warmer months. Raising the shades brings light and fresh air into the apartment. Lowering them can create a thermal buffer for the home and increase privacy.

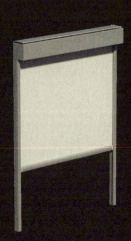

Example: Griesser Solozip® facade awning, seen in the Stendhal housing project, Paris

Contributed by: Studio Muoto, France

# Spread the Load:
## A simple technique uses many smaller wood pieces as support members

Developing countries around the globe are rapidly using up all of their indigenous hardwoods. Constructing reciprocal framework structures allows the use of smaller, younger pieces of wood from timber farms rather than felling old-growth trees for construction. The load is spread out across many smaller members, so none need the strength typical of support beams. While the technique requires some engineering skills, assembly on-site is simple and can often be done without complex machinery.

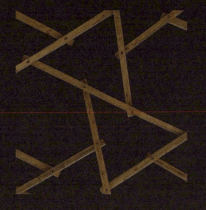

Example: Wood support members seen at Mkombozi Primary School, Chamazi, Tanzania

Contributed by: Gunter Klix, Tanzania

# Don't Overcook the Bricks: Sometimes, "good enough" is sufficient—and sustainable

Bricks cooked at low temperatures typically aren't as strong as those fired at higher temperatures. But they are usually strong enough for buildings up to a certain height—and they're cost-efficient. So their sustainability lies in matching the material to the need, and not adding strength—and cost—where it's not needed. An added benefit: the lower cooking temperature means they're more porous than bricks made in hotter ovens, so they offer superior humidity regulation. And if they're made locally, the environmental impact of transporting them can be minimized.

Example: Perforated brick from Cerámica Tejala, seen in House 712, Gualba, Spain

Contributed by: Harquitectes, Spain

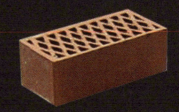

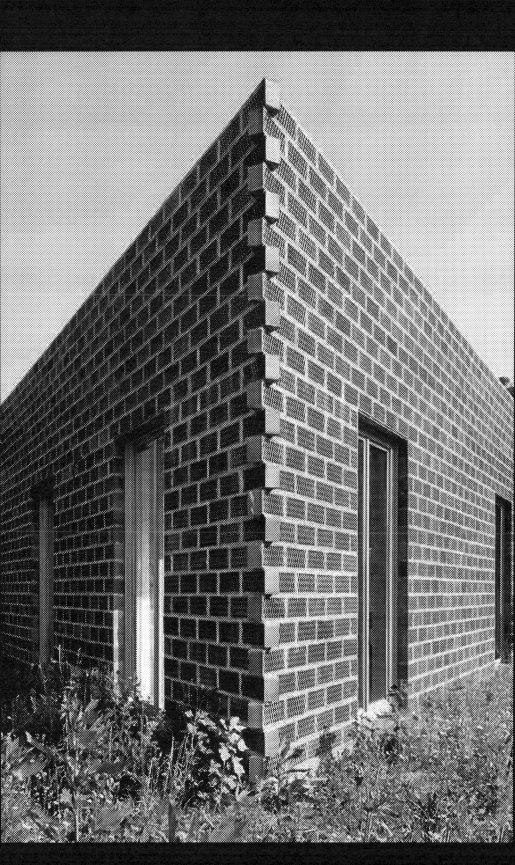

# Build with Mushrooms:
# Bricks made from agricultural waste offer a possible alternative to styrofoam

Mycelium brick is a compostable building material cultivated from agricultural waste. With the rootlike structure of mushrooms, it can be grown into almost any form, and when dried can be used as a water-, mold-, and fire-resistant building material. With a compressive strength of about 30 psi—less than 1 percent of what concrete typically has—it cannot replace concrete in traditional buildings. But it weighs about 8% of concrete, and it suggests new possibilities for lightweight sustainable structures. It also insulates well, and it can serve as an alternative to oil-based insulation.

Example: Mycelium brick by The Living, Ecovative, Arup, and Big Compost, seen in MoMA PS1 Pavilion, New York

Contributed by: David Benjamin (The Living), USA

# Frescos for the Modern Era:
# A low-maintenance, nontoxic alternative to mineral-oil-based paints

Keim is a silicate-based paint that can be absorbed by plaster in a manner reminiscent of fresco paintings from antiquity. While the basic concept—combining paint and substrate by silification—was developed more than 150 years ago, it's an idea that remains valid today. Because the paint doesn't sit on top of the surface but rather permeates the material, it appears very deep. The mineral pigments make the colors UV-resistant, giving them great durability with relatively little maintenance and making them a good alternative to high performance mineral-oil-based paints.

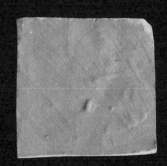

Example: Keim Granital ® in color 9550

Contributed by: Johnston Marklee, USA

# Holy Concrete!
# Hollowing out sections can reduce the material needed by up to 60 percent

Building elements affected by bending—for instance, slabs and beams—rarely use materials efficiently. It's hard to minimize weight by changing the shape of these elements, and it's often impractical because unusual forms are difficult to integrate into designs. An alternative approach developed by Werner Sobek instead seeks to reshape these elements from the inside. Low-stress areas of the concrete can effectively be hollowed out with spherical voids in various sizes, while parts that face greater stress remain solid—and therefore stronger. This strategy can reduce mass by as much as 60 percent without reducing load-bearing capabilities.

Example: Concept of gradation by the use of mineral hollow spheres (left: sphere packing, right: concrete structure), developed at ILEK, University of Stuttgart, Germany

Contributed by: Institute for Lightweight Structures and Conceptual Design (ILEK), University of Stuttgart, Germany

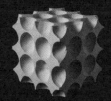

# Be Reasonable:
# Standard wood elements sized
# to do what they need to do

This weekend home in Viggsö, Sweden, was designed so that a single person could carry all the materials needed from a drop-off area by the shoreline to the site on a cliff some fifty meters above the water. The main structure, made of 11.5-centimeter-thick laminated timber, was set up in three days and became the base for all further construction. The goal was to create sustainability by using only the amount of material that was strictly necessary, showing how simple, standard components can become architecture.

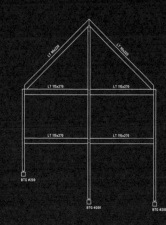

Example: Standard laminated wood beams and pillars, seen in AF. 82 / Viggsö / 1310, Viggsö, Sweden

Contributed by: Arrhov Frick, Sweden

# Easy on the Ears:
# A sliding wall that's good for acoustics (and the environment)

Fast-growing but sturdy, rattan has been used for thousands of years for furniture and as a finish for lightweight walls and doors. The rough, woven surface structure is effective at sound insulation, making it especially suitable for small buildings. And since it's a liana—a woody vine—rattan can play a role in forest maintenance, providing a profitable crop for loggers that can be harvested more frequently than the trees it grows on.

Example: Closed rattan cane webbing
No2 by Rodeka, seen in House Heyvaert,
Destelbergen, Belgium

Contributed by: CRIT / Peter Swinnen,
Belgium

# Embrace the Breeze:
## If the climate is right, your living room might be better off without a window

Sustainability can depend on finding smart alternatives to even the most basic elements. In apartments for teachers at a private school in Tanzania, APC decided to use conventional air-conditioning only in the bedrooms. The living rooms and public areas have higher ceilings and openings on at least two sides with a combination of glass slats and netting, which lets the breeze in but keeps the critters out.

Example: Breezway, seen in International School of Tanganyika, Dar es Salaam

Contributed by: APC Architectural Pioneering Consultants, Tanzania

# Call the Local Tile Maker:
# A traditional material offers a smart alternative for future construction

Tiles have been used for walls, floors, and roofs for millennia, and yet they're as sustainable and future-proof as just about any building material. They're made from a widely available natural material—clay—and are resistant to environmental factors such as UV radiation, temperature swings, and saltwater. These qualities have long been utilized by small-batch producers who perfect methods of forming, painting, glazing, and cooking tiles that suit local needs. Keeping these manufacturers alive makes it possible for designers to work closely with producers and efficiently use the properties of a specific tile.

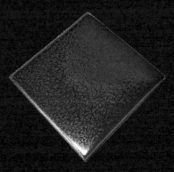

Example: Tailor-made glazed ceramic tile from Royal Tichelaar Ceramics, seen in Park Pavilion, National Park de Hoge Veluwe, The Netherlands

Contributed by: Monadnock, The Netherlands

# A Smaller Toilet:
# Saving space in the bathroom
# can alleviate building bloat

With the size of houses in Western countries rapidly increasing, one simple path toward more sustainable construction is building less and using space more efficiently. A logical place to do that is the bathroom, where economizing on space is typically less noticeable than in, say, the living room. And an easy way to accomplish this is using a shorter toilet, or what the trades dub "guest toilets." This toilet requires eight centimeters less depth than a standard bowl, a 14 percent reduction.

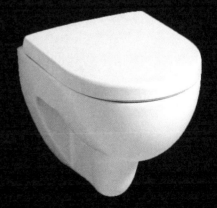

Example: Keramag Renova Nr. 1 Comprimo, seen in Flottwell Zwei, Berlin

Contributed by: Heide & von Beckerath, Germany

# Screw It, Don't Glue It:
# Prepare for disaster by choosing simple materials that can easily be reassembled

A big part of sustainability is anticipating the kinds of damage your building might endure —especially in seismic areas—so it's smart to avoid products that will be difficult to find or replace when something breaks. That means using reliable building materials and avoiding glues. Since things that are glued together are often impossible to separate, in case of damage you may end up having to replace far more than the elements needing repair. The 57-story Torre Reforma in Mexico City did not use any glues but instead screwable pedestals as a floor system and polished concrete walls in all interiors.

Example: DPH pedestals from recycled polypropylene, by Buzon, seen in Torre Reforma, Mexico City

Contributed by: Benjamín Romano (LBR&A), Mexico

# The Power of Nothing:
## Sometimes not building is the right thing to do

The most sustainable material is no material at all. No natural resources are consumed. No energy is used. No emissions are released. No waste is produced. But using no materials means not building, or adapting what's already there. That can mean delay, postponement, or non-planning instead of designing and building. Or it can mean determining how we can best use a given space and the resources we fill it with. It might mean getting creative and using an existing or planned structure to serve multiple purposes. Each project must be individually assessed, minimized, and adjusted to meet the needs of various users. Anthony Froshaug's visual method, first developed in the 1950s, helps achieve those goals—and that's the key to sustainability.

Example: Graph from Anthony Froshaug's *ulm*, no. 4, 1959, pp. 63–65

Contributed by: Jesko Fezer, Germany

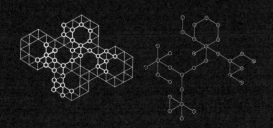

|  |  |  |
|---|---|---|
| 7. Rampe; | 7. ramp; | 7. rampe; |
| 8. Treppenabsatz; | 8. landing; | 8. palier; |
| 9. Rampe; | 9. ramp; | 9. rampe; |
| 10. Praxiseingang; | 10. patients' entrance; | 10. entrée du cabinet; |
| 11. Wartezimmer; | 11. waiting room; | 11. salle d'attente; |
| 12. Behandlungszimmer; | 12. surgery; | 12. salle de traitement; |
| 13. WC; | 13. wc; | 13. toilette; |
| 14. Hausangestelltenzimmer; | 14. maid's room; | 14. chambres de bonnes; |
| 15. Wohnungseingang; | 15. house entrance; | 15. entrée de l'appartement; |
| 16. Treppe; | 16. stairs; | 16. escalier; |
| 17. Treppenabsatz; | 17. landing; | 17. palier; |
| 18. WC; | 18. wc; | 18. toilette; |
| 19. Küchenvorraum; | 19. kitchen passage; | 19. antichambre; |
| 20. Küche; | 20. kitchen; | 20. cuisine; |
| 21. Vorratskammer; | 21. store room; | 21. office; |
| 22. Eßzimmer; | 22. dining room; | 22. salle à manger; |
| 23. Salon; | 23. living room; | 23. salon; |
| 24. Salon; | 24. living room; | 24. salon; |
| 25. Terrasse; | 25. terrace; | 25. terrasse; |
| 26. Treppe; | 26. stairs; | 26. escalier; |
| 27. Flur; | 27. passage; | 27. couloir; |
| 28. Schlafzimmer; | 28. bedroom; | 28. chambre à coucher; |
| 29. Bad; | 29. bathroom; | 29. salle de bains; |
| 30. Schlafzimmer; | 30. bedroom; | 30. chambre à coucher; |
| 31. Schlafzimmer; | 31. bedroom; | 31. chambre à coucher; |
| 32. Bad. | 32. bathroom. | 32. salle de bains. |

Die möglichen Kommunikationswege stellen sich in folgender Matrix (6.5) dar. Aus Gründen der besseren Übersichtlichkeit sind die Nullen hier durch Punkte ersetzt worden.

The circulation relationships can be shown in the following matrix (6.5). To make this matrix more legible, the zero signs are replaced by dots.

Les voies de communication possibles sont représentées dans la matrice suivante (6.5). Pour plus de clarté, on a remplacé ici les zéros par des points.

| | 1 | 2 | 3 | 4 | 5 | 6 | 7 | 8 | 9 | 10 | 11 | 12 | 13 | 14 | 15 | 16 | 17 | 18 | 19 | 20 | 21 | 22 | 23 | 24 | 25 | 26 | 27 | 28 | 29 | 30 | 31 | 32 | $S_i$ |
|---|---|---|---|---|---|---|---|---|---|---|---|---|---|---|---|---|---|---|---|---|---|---|---|---|---|---|---|---|---|---|---|---|---|
| 1 | 0 | . | . | 1 | . | . | . | . | . | . | . | . | . | . | . | . | . | . | . | . | . | . | . | . | . | . | . | . | . | . | . | . | 1 |
| 2 | . | 0 | . | 1 | . | . | . | . | . | . | . | . | . | . | . | . | . | . | . | . | . | . | . | . | . | . | . | . | . | . | . | . | 1 |
| 3 | . | . | 0 | 1 | . | . | . | . | . | . | . | . | . | . | . | . | . | . | . | . | . | . | . | . | . | . | . | . | . | . | . | . | 1 |
| 4 | 1 | 1 | 1 | 0 | 1 | . | 1 | . | . | . | . | . | . | . | . | . | . | . | . | . | . | . | . | . | . | . | . | . | . | . | . | . | 5 |
| 5 | . | . | . | 1 | 0 | 1 | . | . | . | . | . | . | . | . | . | . | . | . | . | . | . | . | . | . | . | . | . | . | . | . | . | . | 2 |
| 6 | . | . | . | . | 1 | 0 | . | . | . | . | . | . | . | . | . | . | . | . | . | . | . | . | . | . | . | . | . | . | . | . | . | . | 1 |
| 7 | . | . | . | 1 | . | . | 0 | 1 | . | . | . | . | . | . | . | . | . | . | . | . | . | . | . | . | . | . | . | . | . | . | . | . | 2 |
| 8 | . | . | . | . | . | . | 1 | 0 | 1 | . | . | . | . | . | 1 | . | . | . | . | . | . | . | . | . | . | . | . | . | . | . | . | . | 3 |
| 9 | . | . | . | . | . | . | . | 1 | 0 | 1 | . | . | . | . | . | . | . | . | . | . | . | . | . | . | . | . | . | . | . | . | . | . | 2 |
| 10 | . | . | . | . | . | . | . | . | 1 | 0 | 1 | 1 | 1 | 1 | . | . | . | . | . | . | . | . | . | . | . | . | . | . | . | . | . | . | 5 |
| 11 | . | . | . | . | . | . | . | . | . | 1 | 0 | 1 | . | . | . | . | . | . | . | . | . | . | . | . | . | . | . | . | . | . | . | . | 2 |
| 12 | . | . | . | . | . | . | . | . | . | 1 | 1 | 0 | . | . | . | . | . | . | . | . | . | . | . | . | . | . | . | . | . | . | . | . | 2 |
| 13 | . | . | . | . | . | . | . | . | . | 1 | . | . | 0 | . | . | . | . | . | . | . | . | . | . | . | . | . | . | . | . | . | . | . | 1 |
| 14 | . | . | . | . | . | . | . | . | . | 1 | . | . | . | 0 | . | . | . | . | . | . | . | . | . | . | . | . | . | . | . | . | . | . | 1 |
| 15 | . | . | . | . | . | . | . | 1 | . | . | . | . | . | . | 0 | 1 | . | . | . | . | . | . | . | . | . | . | . | . | . | . | . | . | 2 |
| 16 | . | . | . | . | . | . | . | . | . | . | . | . | . | . | 1 | 0 | 1 | . | . | . | . | . | . | . | . | . | . | . | . | . | . | . | 2 |
| 17 | . | . | . | . | . | . | . | . | . | . | . | . | . | . | . | 1 | 0 | 1 | 1 | . | . | 1 | 1 | . | . | . | . | . | . | . | . | . | 5 |
| 18 | . | . | . | . | . | . | . | . | . | . | . | . | . | . | . | . | 1 | 0 | . | . | . | . | . | . | . | . | . | . | . | . | . | . | 1 |
| 19 | . | . | . | . | . | . | . | . | . | . | . | . | . | . | . | . | 1 | . | 0 | 1 | . | . | . | . | . | . | . | . | . | . | . | . | 2 |
| 20 | . | . | . | . | . | . | . | . | . | . | . | . | . | . | . | . | . | . | 1 | 0 | 1 | . | . | . | . | . | . | . | . | . | . | . | 2 |
| 21 | . | . | . | . | . | . | . | . | . | . | . | . | . | . | . | . | . | . | . | 1 | 0 | 1 | . | . | . | . | . | . | . | . | . | . | 2 |
| 22 | . | . | . | . | . | . | . | . | . | . | . | . | . | . | . | . | 1 | . | . | . | 1 | 0 | 1 | . | . | . | . | . | . | . | . | . | 3 |
| 23 | . | . | . | . | . | . | . | . | . | . | . | . | . | . | . | . | 1 | . | . | . | . | 1 | 0 | 1 | . | . | . | . | . | . | . | . | 3 |
| 24 | . | . | . | . | . | . | . | . | . | . | . | . | . | . | . | . | . | . | . | . | . | . | 1 | 0 | 1 | 1 | . | . | . | . | . | . | 3 |
| 25 | . | . | . | . | . | . | . | . | . | . | . | . | . | . | . | . | . | . | . | . | . | . | . | 1 | 0 | . | . | . | . | . | . | . | 1 |
| 26 | . | . | . | . | . | . | . | . | . | . | . | . | . | . | . | . | . | . | . | . | . | . | . | 1 | . | 0 | 1 | 1 | . | . | . | . | 3 |
| 27 | . | . | . | . | . | . | . | . | . | . | . | . | . | . | . | . | . | . | . | . | . | . | . | . | . | 1 | 0 | 1 | . | 1 | 1 | . | 4 |
| 28 | . | . | . | . | . | . | . | . | . | . | . | . | . | . | . | . | . | . | . | . | . | . | . | . | . | 1 | 1 | 0 | 1 | . | . | . | 3 |
| 29 | . | . | . | . | . | . | . | . | . | . | . | . | . | . | . | . | . | . | . | . | . | . | . | . | . | . | . | 1 | 0 | . | . | . | 1 |
| 30 | . | . | . | . | . | . | . | . | . | . | . | . | . | . | . | . | . | . | . | . | . | . | . | . | . | . | 1 | . | . | 0 | . | . | 1 |
| 31 | . | . | . | . | . | . | . | . | . | . | . | . | . | . | . | . | . | . | . | . | . | . | . | . | . | . | 1 | . | . | . | 0 | 1 | 2 |
| 32 | . | . | . | . | . | . | . | . | . | . | . | . | . | . | . | . | . | . | . | . | . | . | . | . | . | . | . | . | . | . | 1 | 0 | 1 |

Die maximale Zeilensumme beträgt 5; also braucht man ein Raster, bei dem in jedem Punkt mindestens fünf Verbindungslinien münden. Damit scheiden die Rastertypen

The maximum row sum equals 5; this implies that each point of the grid must have a minimum of 5 connections. This eliminates

La somme maximum pour une ligne est de 5; il faut donc que cinq liaisons au moins aboutissent à chaque point de la trame choisie. Ce qui élimine, dans notre cas,

# Donor Acknowledgment

This book is inspired by the 6th LafargeHolcim Forum for Sustainable Construction, which was dedicated to the theme of "Re-materializing Construction" and held at the American University in Cairo in 2019. The forum created an interdisciplinary platform for exchanging ideas and information for 350 experts from 55 countries — with keynote speeches, workshops, and site visits focused on strategies to reduce consumption throughout the material cycle from extraction to processing, transport, installation, maintenance, and removal.

The series of conferences on the topic of sustainable construction brings together specialists of all generations from architecture, engineering, urban planning, materials science, construction technology, and related fields to exchange information on creating a built environment that advances sustainable development.

The triennial forum is an initiative of the LafargeHolcim Foundation for Sustainable Construction based in Zurich, Switzerland. The foundation also conducts the LafargeHolcim Awards — the world's most significant competition for sustainable design. Every three years, the competition seeks leading projects of professionals as well as bold ideas from the next generation that combine sustainable construction solutions with architectural excellence.

www.lafargeholcim-foundation.org

The LafargeHolcim Foundation promotes sustainability throughout building and construction and is sponsored by LafargeHolcim and its operational companies in around eighty countries. LafargeHolcim is the global leader in building materials and solutions, pursuing innovation along the entire value chain from processes to products, from quarry to worksite.

www.lafargeholcim.com

**LafargeHolcimFoundation**
for Sustainable Construction

An initiative of
**LafargeHolcim**

# Contributor Biographies

Achilles Ahimbisibwe
is an architect, Transsolar Academy
fellow in Stuttgart, and lecturer in the
Department of Architecture at Uganda
Martyrs University. He was a research
assistant engaged in the Supporting
African Municipalities in Sustainable
Energy Transitions and Energy & Low-
Income Tropical Housing projects, and
participated in assessing local construction
materials in Kenya and Rwanda under the
Joint Development of Courses for Energy
Efficiently & Sustainable Housing in Africa.
Ahimbisibwe has experience engaging
local communities, sensitizing people,
and informing policies on sustainable
technologies and construction practices.

Marilyne Andersen
is professor of sustainable construction
technologies and head of the Laboratory
of Integrated Performance in Design at
the Swiss Federal Institute of Technology
in Lausanne. She was dean of the School
of Architecture, Civil & Environmental
Engineering from 2013 to 2018 and is
the chair of the Scientific Commission
for the development of the Smart
Living Lab in Fribourg, Switzerland.
She has been an associate professor in
the Building Technology Group of the
School of Architecture & Planning at the
Massachusetts Institute of Technology
and head of the MIT Daylighting Lab,
which she founded in 2004. Andersen
holds a master of science in psychics
and specialized in daylighting through
her PhD in building physics at EPFL in
the Solar Energy & Building Physics
Laboratory and as a visiting scholar in the
Building Technologies Department of the
Lawrence Berkeley National Laboratory
in California.

Marc Angélil
is professor of architecture and design at
ETH Zurich. His research on social and
spatial developments of metropolitan
regions worldwide has led to a number of
publications, which include *Indizien*, on
the political economy of contemporary
territories; *Cidade de Deus!*, on informal
housing in Rio de Janeiro; *Cities of Change
Addis Ababa*, on urban transformation
in developing countries; and *Mirroring
Effects: Tales of Territory*, cowritten with
Cary Siress, which analyzes contemporary
political and economic practices concerning
environment-making. He is a practicing
architect at agps architecture, with offices
in Los Angeles and Zurich.

Alpha Yacob Arsano
is a PhD candidate and research assistant at
the Massachusetts Institute of Technology.
She is an architect with a great interest in
maximizing passive building strategies
in different climatic conditions, and
she studies the potential of natural
ventilation in buildings, thermal comfort
of occupants, and effect of climate change
in various climates around the globe.
She completed her bachelor of science in
architecture at the Ethiopian Institute of
Architecture, Building Construction & City
Development.

Yunus Ballim
is deputy vice-chancellor of the
University of the Witwatersrand (Wits)
in Johannesburg and vice-chancellor and
principal of Sol Plaatje University in
Kimberley, South Africa. He graduated
with a bachelor of science in civil
engineering and worked as a site engineer
on bridges and projects including the
Daspoort Cutting near Hartbeespoort.

He returned to Wits for a master of engineering and a PhD.

Cristián Calvo Barentin
studied architecture at the Technical University Federico Santa María of Valparaíso, Chile. After working as an architect, he cofounded an electronic development firm, where he worked as an interaction designer. His passion for R&D brought him back to Federico Santa María in 2012, where he has served as a teaching and research assistant and helped introduce industrial robot arms in an advanced architectural design studio for the first time in a South American architecture school. His research focuses on the development of digitally driven prefabrication systems, mass customization, physical computing, digital fabrication, and parametric design.

Elise Berodier
is a scientist and project leader in the Laboratory of Construction & Architecture at the Swiss Federal Institute of Technology (EPFL) in Fribourg. She obtained her doctorate in material science from EPFL. After her PhD, she worked for GCP Applied Technologies, a leading manufacturer of admixtures for cement and concrete. She has worked with the Swiss Agency for Development & Cooperation in Haiti, where she met multiple actors in the construction sector in the attempt to identify barriers to good practice in concrete making. She is also involved in the Low Carbon Cementitious Initiative, which promotes eco-cementitious materials.

Christine Binswanger
is senior partner at Herzog & de Meuron. She is responsible for many international projects, with particular focus on Switzerland, France, Spain, and the United States. The Herzog & de Meuron partnership has grown to be an office with over 450 people worldwide. In addition to their headquarters in Basel, they have offices in London, Berlin, Copenhagen, New York, and Hong Kong. Binswanger studied architecture at the ETH Zurich and received the Meret Oppenheim Prize in 2004 in recognition of her active leadership in the architecture and art community.

Philippe Block
is professor of architecture and structure at ETH Zurich, Switzerland. He codirects the Block Research Group with Tom Van Mele, is director of the Swiss National Centre of Competence in Research in Digital Fabrication, and is founding partner of Ochsendorf DeJong & Block. He holds a PhD in building technology from MIT, and worked as a visiting researcher at the Royal Danish Academy of Arts in Copenhagen and at the Institute for Lightweight Structures & Conceptual Design, University of Stuttgart. Block has been awarded the Rössler Prize, Hangai Prize, the Tsuboi Award from the International Association of Shell & Spatial Structures, the Edoardo Benvenuto prize for "scientific research on the history of structural mechanics and art of building," and the Berlin Art Prize for Architecture. His work has been exhibited at the Design Triennial 2009 in New York and the 13th International Architecture Biennale in Venice in 2012.

Lord Norman Foster
is chairman and founder of Foster + Partners in London. He graduated

from Manchester University School of Architecture and City Planning and won a Henry Fellowship to Yale University, where he was a fellow of Jonathan Edwards College and gained a master's degree in Architecture. Foster has been awarded the Royal Gold Medal for Architecture, the Gold Medal for the French Academy of Architecture, the American Institute of Architects Gold Medal, and the Praemium Imperiale in Tokyo, and he was appointed Officer of the Order of Arts and Letters by the Ministry of Culture in France. In 1999 he won the Pritzker Architecture Prize, and in 2002 he was elected to the German Orden Pour le Mérite für Wissenschaften und Künste. In 1990 he was granted a knighthood in the Queen's Birthday Honours List, and in 1997 he was appointed by the Queen to the Order of Merit. In 1999 Foster was honored with a life peerage in the Queen's Birthday Honours List, taking the title Lord Foster of Thames Bank.

Maarten Gielen
is designer, manager, and researcher of Rotor, a Brussels collective of people sharing a common interest in material flows in industry and construction. Together with Lionel Devlieger, he was curator of the 2013 Oslo Architecture Triennale, "Behind the Green Door: Architecture and the Desire for Sustainability." In 2012 he was appointed visiting professor at the Geneva University of Art & Design. He was awarded the young Maaskant prize in 2015 and the Schelling Architecture prize in 2018, for working on changing the way materials are used in architecture and construction engineering.

Harry Gugger
is principal of Harry Gugger Studio in Basel, and professor of architectural and urban design at the Swiss Federal Institute of Technology in Lausanne, where he directs the Laboratory Basel, dedicated to territorial, urban, and architectural design. The laboratory was in charge of the national participation of Bahrain "Reclaim" at the 12th International Architecture Biennale in Venice in 2010, winning the Golden Lion award. He commenced a nineteen-year collaboration with Herzog & de Meuron in 1990. He was a partner in the firm, and his last projects included CaixaForum in Madrid and the Tate Modern Extension in London.

Guillaume Habert
is professor of sustainable construction at ETH Zurich. He was previously a research engineer at the Université de Paris-Est and has a PhD in geology from the Université de Toulouse. He has completed postdoctoral studies on low-cost construction materials at Universidade Federal da Paraíba, Brazil. Habert received the 2015 Robert L'Hermite Medal from RILEM (International Union of Laboratories and Experts in Construction Materials, Systems & Structures) for his work on the environmental analysis of building materials and processes along with his contribution to the development and understanding of alternative materials such as geopolymers and recycled products.

Dirk Hebel
is professor of sustainable construction at the Karlsruhe Institut für Technologie. He was principal investigator at the Future Cities Laboratory of ETH Zurich

and Singapore's National Research Foundation. He obtained a master of architecture from ETH Zurich and from Princeton University and was assistant professor of architecture and construction and director of the Master of Advanced Studies program in Urban Design at ETH Zurich and founding scientific director of the Ethiopian Institute of Architecture Building Construction & City Development in Addis Ababa. Hebel practices architecture with his firm, DRKH Architecture.

Felix Heisel
is a partner at 2hs Architekten und Ingenieur PartGmbB and head of research at the Department of Sustainable Construction of the Karlsruhe Institut für Technologie and the Future Cities Laboratory in Singapore. Beginning in 2020, Heisel will be assistant professor of architecture and circular construction at Cornell University, Ithaca, NY. He has taught at Harvard GSD, ETH Zurich, EiABC Addis Ababa, the Berlage Institute Rotterdam, and the University of the Arts Berlin, where he earned a master of architecture. He has received the JEC Asia Innovation Award, Ministry of Education Innovation Grant Singapore, Zumtobel Group Award, Swiss KTI project fund, Smart Innovation Grant Singapore, and the Bauhaus.Solar Award.

Anna Heringer
is honorary professor of the UNESCO Chair in Earthen Architecture, Construction Cultures, and Sustainable Development at the Grenoble School of Architecture. She is a visiting professor at the Technical University Vienna, and she teaches a design studio on earthen architecture at the ETH

Zurich together with Martin Rauch. She has been a visiting professor at universities in Stuttgart, Linz, Vienna, and Alghero. Heringer studied architecture at the University of Arts and Industrial Design in Linz, and has received a Loeb Fellowship at the Harvard Graduate School of Design.

Laila Iskandar
is former minister of urban renewal and informal settlements in Egypt. She has worked as a researcher, speaker, and consultant with governmental and international agencies as well as with the private sector in the fields of gender, education and development, environment, child labor, and governance. Her consulting work encompasses grassroots issues and policy matters. Iskandar was a consultant to the minister of environment on solid-waste management issues in Egypt. She has worked with the informal waste sector for over thirty years and has designed, developed, and implemented community solid-waste projects. Iskandar studied economics, political science, and business at Cairo University. She holds a master of arts in teaching from the University of California, Berkeley, and a doctorate in education from Columbia University.

Heba Allah Essam E. Khalil
is professor of sustainable urbanism in the Department of Architecture of Cairo University's Faculty of Engineering. She teaches and conducts research in community development, informal areas, and integrated urban systems, focusing on urban metabolism and improving micro-climates in cities through meta-flow analysis, simulation, and participatory action research. She has worked as an architect, urban planner, and housing

expert with multiscale agencies, authorities, and clients both local and international. She has worked for international organizations including the World Bank and UN-Habitat. Khalil holds a PhD in architectural engineering from Cairo University and has served as adjunct professor in architectural design at MIT.

Bruce King
is director of the Ecological Building Network in San Rafael, CA, which promotes and fosters building to favor intelligent design, clean energy, and healthy materials. It is a nonprofit coalition of engineers, builders, and architects developing and disseminating best technologies for the built environment. He has served as a green/clean technology advisor to start-ups and other organizations and has worked on high-rise structures in San Francisco, aircraft remodeling in Miami, resorts in Tahiti, Buddhist monasteries in the Colorado Rockies, passive solar design, and stand-alone houses. He was previously a consulting structural engineer in private practice and an engineer at Skidmore Owings & Merrill.

Christoph Küffer
is professor of urban ecology in the Department of Landscape Architecture at the University of Applied Sciences of Eastern Switzerland. He is also a lecturer in the Department of Architecture and a senior scientist in the Department of Environmental Systems Science at ETH Zurich. He studied environmental science at ETH Zurich, completing his PhD in plant ecology. He has experience in collaborating with social scientists, humanities scholars, and artists. He has served as a fellow at the transdisciplinary laboratory Collegium

Helveticum, the Center for Interdisciplinary Research at Bielefeld University, and as a cochair of Environmental Humanities Switzerland. His research focuses on urban ecology, biodiversity conservation in human-dominated ecosystems, and the impact of global change on island and mountain ecosystems.

Anne Lacaton
is principal of Lacaton & Vassal Architectes in Paris and an associate professor of architecture and design at ETH Zurich. Lacaton & Vassal received the French Grand Prix National d'Architecture in 2008. The practice has won the Erich Schelling Award, International Fellowship of the Royal Institute of British Architects, Daylight and building components of the Velum Foundation, Heinrich Tessenow Gold Medal, and the Mies van der Rohe Award. Lacaton has served as visiting professor at the University of Madrid, Swiss Federal Institute of Technology Lausanne, University of Florida, University at Buffalo, New York, and the Harvard Graduate School of Design.

Soumen Maity
is senior general manager and assistant vice president at Development Alternatives in New Delhi, a social enterprise dedicated to sustainable development. He leads the technology management business of Technology & Action for Rural Advancement. His expertise lies in the building material sector wherein he has been instrumental in exploring commercial approaches to the utilization of industrial waste, improving energy efficiency and reducing environmental emissions. He has undertaken feasibility studies for the

introduction of cleaner brick production in Afghanistan, Bangladesh, Indonesia, Nepal, and Vietnam. Maity obtained a PhD in materials science from the Central Glass & Ceramic Research Institute.

Sarah Nichols
will begin serving as assistant professor for technology and architecture at Rice University in Houston in 2020. Currently she is a visiting studio critic at Rice and a doctoral candidate at the Institute for History & Theory of Architecture at ETH Zurich. She holds an Advanced Master of Architecture from the Berlage Institute in Rotterdam and a Bachelor of Science in Architecture from the University of Michigan. Sarah has also led design studios and seminar courses in architecture and urban design and works independently as an architect.

John Orr
is university lecturer in concrete structures and an Engineering & Physical Sciences Research Council Early Career Fellow at the University of Cambridge, United Kingdom. Orr graduated with a first-class MEng(hons) degree in civil engineering from the University of Bath. He completed a PhD in fabric formwork at the University of Bath. He was previously director of research and assistant professor in civil engineering at the University of Bath, and joined the University of Cambridge in 2017. He is the author of *Structural Innovation in Europe* (University of Bath, 2010) and his work has been published in journals, including: *Construction & Building Materials*; *Engineering Structures*; *European Journal of Computational Mechanics*; *Resources, Conservation*

*& Recycling*; *Structural Engineer*; and *Structures*.

Noelle Paulson
is a member of the Block Research Group at ETH Zurich. She is coauthor of *Beyond Bending: Reimagining Compression Shells*, together with Philippe Block, Tom Van Mele, and Matthias Rippmann. A graduate of St. Olaf College and Washington University in St. Louis, Paulson completed master and doctoral degrees in nineteenth-century European art history. She has worked as a freelance art-historical writer, editor, and consultant.

Eva Pfannes
is director of Ooze Architects, a Rotterdam firm that she founded in 2003 with Sylvain Hartenberg. She has been a tutor and guest critic at the North London Polytechnic and the Art Academy in Stuttgart, has taught at the Eindhoven Design Academy, and has been practitioner in residence at Central Saint Martins – University of the Arts London. Pfannes has won the Dutch Basis Prix de Rome for Architecture, the British Landscape Institute Award for the best "Design for a Temporary Landscape" with the King's Cross Pond Club, and the LafargeHolcim Awards Bronze for Latin America for "Urban Circulatory System in Brazil."

Albert Pope
is a professor in the Rice University School of Architecture in Houston, TX. He is also founding director of Present Future, a design program and think tank at Rice. He has written and lectured extensively on postwar urban development and he is currently studying the urban implications of

climate change. He is engaged in research on carbon neutral urban development, producing large-scale planning projects for Houston and Detroit. He obtained a bachelor of architecture from SCI-Arc and master of architecture from Princeton University. He has held teaching positions at Yale University and SCI-Arc.

Mariana Popescu
is a PhD researcher at the Block Research Group at ETH Zurich. She studied architecture at Delft University of Technology, specializing in non-standard and interactive architecture. After graduating she joined Hive Systems, a start-up developing a platform enabling designers and architects to quickly conceptualize, visualize, and build complex interactive environments using distributed algorithms. She was an architect specializing in parametric design at Zwarts & Jansma Architects, Amsterdam. She served on the Nuon Solar Team, which designed, built, and raced a solar car across the Australian outback, and was part of the ReVolt House team, which built a fully self-sustaining house.

Francesco Ranaudo
is an architect and chartered structural engineer specialized in tall building design, structural optimization, and performance-based seismic design. In 2013 he earned a double master's degree with honors in architecture and building engineering at the University of Naples Federico II. In 2015 he honed his structural engineering knowledge with a second-level master degree in emerging technologies for construction at the University of Naples and the University of California. He has worked for Skidmore, Owings and Merrill in San Francisco and London. In 2017 he joined the Institute for Lightweight Structures and Conceptual Design at University of Stuttgart as a research assistant and was the main author and developer of the topology optimization software ATOMuS. Since October 2018 Ranaudo has been a PhD candidate at ETH Zurich, where he is a research assistant in the Block Research Group and NCCR Digital Fabrication.

Loreta Castro Reguera
is design director and founder of Taller Capital in Mexico City and a professor in the School of Architecture at the Universidad Nacional Autónoma de México. Her focus is on the design of infrastructural public spaces to better manage water through urban design. She has been awarded a Fulbright Scholarship and the CEMEX Marcelo Zambrano prize. She was also recipient of a Young Creators Program Fellowship and a Druker Traveling Fellowship Award at Harvard's Graduate School of Design. She was the design director and technical coordinator of the UNAM project "Hydropuncture" in Mexico City, which received a Global LafargeHolcim Awards Gold in 2018.

Matthias Rippmann
was a senior scientist at the Block Research Group at ETH Zurich. He studied architecture at the University of Stuttgart and the University of Melbourne. He worked for the Institute for Lightweight Structures and Conceptual Design at the University of Stuttgart and Werner Sobek Engineering in Stuttgart. In 2010 he cofounded the architecture and consultancy firm ROK – Rippmann Oesterle Knauss

in Zurich. His doctoral thesis was awarded the ETH medal for outstanding dissertations. Rippmann died in August 2019.

Phil Ross
is an artist, inventor, scholar, and cofounder and CTO of MycoWorks in San Francisco. Founded in 2013, MycoWorks produces weatherproof materials using fungi grown from the roots of mushrooms, which are used in footwear, batteries, and automobiles. He studied fine arts at the San Francisco Art Institute and Stanford University. His work has been showcased by New York's Museum of Modern Art, the Los Angeles County Museum of Art, Carnegie Mellon University, Silicon Valley's Zero1, the Moscow Biennale, and Kunsthalle Düsseldorf. His mycelium furniture won Ars Electronica's Award of Distinction for Hybrid Art.

Andreas Ruby
is an architecture journalist, curator, and book publisher. He was born in Dresden in 1966 and studied art history at the University of Cologne. He worked as an editor and correspondent for the architectural journals *Daidalos* and *Werk, Bauen + Wohnen*. In 2001, he cofounded textbild, an agency for architectural communication, curated architectural exhibitions, and organized lecture series on contemporary architecture. In 2008, he cofounded the architecture publishing house Ruby Press, where he has since completed more than thirty book projects. Andreas Ruby has also taught architectural theory at Cornell University, the University of Kassel, Graz University of Technology, and ENSAPM in Paris.

Since 2016 he has been director of the Swiss Architecture Museum.

Ilka Ruby
is a Berlin-based publisher and curator on issues surrounding architecture and urbanism. She studied architecture at RWTH Aachen and TU Vienna. In 2001 she cofounded textbild, an office for architectural communication, and in 2008 Ruby Press, a publishing house with a focus on architecture, art, and other cultural practices engaged in the production of space. In addition to her publishing activities, she has developed curatorial projects such as the video installation *Endless Bauhaus* at the Gropius Bau in Berlin; the exhibition *Druot, Lacaton & Vassal—Tour Bois le Prêtre* for the German Architecture Museum in Frankfurt; *Treasures in Disguise*, the pavilion representing Montenegro at the 14th International Architecture Biennale in Venice; *Never Demolish* for the Copenhagen Architecture Festival; and *Together! The New Architecture of the Collective* at the Vitra Design Museum. Ilka Ruby has taught at Cornell University, University of the Arts Berlin, and the Peter Behrens School of Architecture in Düsseldorf.

Serge Salat
is founder and president of the Urban Morphology & Complex Systems Institute in Paris, a professor at the École Spéciale d'Architecture, and a senior advisor to the United Nations Environmental Programme. He is an architect, urban planner, and expert in the field of spatial planning, urban energy planning, urban policy, and finance. He advises international organizations such as the

IPCC, UNEP Sustainable Building & Climate Initiative, development banks, and national and local governments. He holds doctorates in architecture, economics, and history and civilizations from Ecole d'Architecture de Paris La Villette, Université Paris IX Dauphine.

Arno Schlueter
is professor of architecture & building systems at ETH Zurich and a principal investigator at the ETH Zurich Future Cities Lab in Singapore. He and his team focus on sustainable building systems, new adaptive components and their synergetic integration into architecture, and urban design using computational approaches for modeling, analysis, and control. Schlueter studied architecture at the Technical University of Karlsruhe and holds postgraduate degrees in CAAD and a PhD in building systems from ETH Zurich. In 2009, he cofounded the design and engineering office KEOTO.ch, where he is part of the management board. The work of Architecture & Building Systems Group has been published in scientific journals, magazines, and books, and has won international competitions and prizes.

Karen Scrivener
is a professor and the head of the laboratory of construction materials at the Swiss Federal Institute of Technology in Lausanne. She graduated from the University of Cambridge in materials science and completed a PhD at Imperial College in London, where she later was a lecturer and Royal Society research fellow. Scrivener has worked as a researcher at Lafarge in France, serves as editor in chief of the *Cement and Concrete Research* journal, and is the founder and coordinator

of Nanocem, a group that carries out fundamental research on cementitious materials.

Cary Siress
is senior researcher at ETH Zurich. His work on territorial organization at the Future Cities Laboratory in Singapore focuses on global urbanization processes. He is guest professor in urban design at the Nanjing University Graduate School of Architecture and Urban Planning in China. Previous publications include *Archipelagos: A Manual for Peripheral Buenos Aires*, on future growth in Argentina, *Hard Plan — Soft City*, which investigates the "city as designed" versus the "city as used," and *Mirroring Effects: Tales of Territory*, cowritten with Marc Angélil, which analyzes contemporary political and economic practices concerning environment-making.

Werner Sobek
is director of the Institute for Lightweight Structures & Conceptual Design, University of Stuttgart in Germany, and founder of the Werner Sobek Group. He holds the Mies van der Rohe Chair at the Illinois Institute of Technology in Chicago, and has taught at Harvard University, University of Graz, Massachusetts Institute of Technology, Columbia University, the University of Hamburg, the University of Hannover, and the National University of Singapore. Sobek has received the DuPont Benedictus Award, European Gluelam Award, Fritz Schumacher Award, iF Design Award, SEAOI Structural Engineering Award, AIA awards of the American Institute of Architecture, Hugo Häring Award, Fazlur Rahman Khan Medal, and the UIA's Auguste Perret Prize.

Something Fantastic
is an undisciplinary design practice founded
by three architects, Elena Schütz, Julian
Schubert, and Leonard Streich. Their work
includes designing books, exhibitions,
furniture, buildings, and urban development
schemes, as well as writing, lecturing,
and art directing. Currently the firm is
developing a communal housing type called
Possibility House. In 2016 Something
Fantastic was responsible for the design
of the German Pavilion exhibition at the
15th International Architecture Biennale
in Venice. The three partners taught and
directed the  postgraduate program on
urban design at ETH Zurich from 2012 to
2019 and are now directing the Studio for
Immediate Spaces at the Sandberg Instituut,
Amsterdam.

Mark Swilling
is distinguished professor of sustainable
development at the School of Public
Leadership of Stellenbosch University,
South Africa. He is also codirector of the
Center for Complex Systems in Transition
and academic director of the Sustainability
Institute at Stellenbosch University, visiting
professor at the University of Sheffield,
visiting professor at Utrecht University,
Bass Scholar at Yale University, and
board chair of the Development Bank of
Southern Africa. His research involves
sustainable urban planning, policy analysis,
and trans-disciplinary research in South
Africa. He is coordinator of the United
Nations Environment Programme (UNEP)
International Resource Panel's Working
Group on Cities.

Simon Upton
is parliamentary commissioner for the
environment in Wellington, New Zealand.

He was director of the environment
directorate at the Organisation for
Economic Co-operation & Development
(OECD) in Paris and chairman of the
OECD Round Table on Sustainable
Development. He is a Rhodes Scholar with
degrees in English literature, music, and
law from the University of Auckland and
a master of letters in political philosophy
from the University of Oxford. He was
elected to Parliament in New Zealand and
became one of the country's youngest
cabinet ministers in 1990. He held a wide
variety of portfolios including environment,
biosecurity, science & technology, and
health & state services. He was elected to
the Privy Council in 2000 and retired from
politics in 2001.

Tom Van Mele
is senior scientist and codirector at the
Block Research Group at ETH Zurich
and the lead developer of COMPAS, the
open-source computational framework for
collaboration and research in architecture,
structures, and digital fabrication. Van
Mele studied architecture and structural
engineering at the Vrije Universiteit
Brussel in Brussels. He received his PhD
for a dissertation about the design and
analysis of retractable roofs.

Stefanie Weidner
is a research associate at the Institute for
Lightweight Structures & Conceptual
Design, University of Stuttgart. She
has worked at Werner Sobek Design
and Steimle Architekten, Germany, and
Foster + Partners, United Kingdom. She
studied architecture at the University of
Melbourne and architecture and urban
planning at the University of Stuttgart.

# Image Credits

# Colophon

Editors: Ilka Ruby & Andreas Ruby
Design: Something Fantastic
Art Department (Elena Schütz,
Julian Schubert, Leonard Streich
with Maria Weiss)
Associate Editor: Max Bach
Copyediting: Peter Brooks-Sharpe,
Jacqueline Taylor

Bibliographic information published by
Die Deutsche Bibliothek. Die Deutsche
Bibliothek lists this publication in
the Deutsche Nationalbibliographie;
detailed bibliographic data is available
online at http://portal.dnb.de.

Every effort has been made by
the authors and the publishers to
acknowledge all sources and copyright
holders. In the event of any copyright
holder being inadvertently omitted,
please contact the publishers directly.
Please see pages 398–99 for specific
image credits.

Fonts: Univers, Super GT, Times New
Roman, Arial
Papers: Caribic, Pure Offset, Munken
Cream, Munken Polar

Printed in Italy
ISBN 978-3-944074-32-0

www.ruby-press.com
www.lafargeholcim-foundation.org